High Altitude
Gardening

for the
Inter-Mountain West

Julie McDonald

To my friend, Beverlee Cassady, who in 1972, showed me the love of Jesus through chocolate chip cookies and changed my life forever.

This book relates the author's experience in gardening over the last sixty years. She would be the first to declare that she is not an expert. She offers her advice for your entertainment and accrual of knowledge in battling the elements. Ultimately, each gardener makes their own decisions and learns through trial and error.

Table of Contents

INTRODUCTION

If gardening is genetic, I certainly got the genes. My grandparents were both born in Sweden in 1870. In 1887, my grandmother traveled alone to the United States, settling in Galveston, Texas. After surviving the worst natural disaster in U.S. history, the Galveston Hurricane of 1900, and helping rebuild Galveston, the family moved to Arizona. After work on Roosevelt Dam was completed, they settled in Flagstaff, purchasing a half block on the corner of Park and Santa Fe. Part of the money for that purchase came as a gift from a man who was so impressed with my grandparents' work ethic that he wanted to help them. With a small house at one end of the lot, they began to farm the back half. You can still see the beautiful old trees they planted.

My grandfather died unexpectedly on New Year's Day in 1917 when my dad was two-years old. My grandmother was left with six children, ranging in age from two to seventeen. Many people told her she would not be able to properly care for and support six children. She worked her little farm, took in laundry, cleaned homes for affluent families in Flagstaff and sewed clothing for her children after they had gone to bed. The farm provided food for the family and she sold the excess produce to local merchants. She put all six children through college on her income, selling vegeta-

My front yard

bles and doing domestic work.

I think I was born to garden. Growing up in this environment I learned a lot about gardening in Flagstaff, a place with a short growing season. My earliest memories are of plants, flowers and trees. I don't remember ever NOT being interested in them. At age three, I remember my Aunt Julia taking me by the hand out to my grandmother's garden. She showed me a vibrant crocus, telling me, "This is the first flower of spring."

As I grew older, we went on many family picnics in the woods- but not without purpose. Everyone had a gunnysack and everyone filled it with cow pies. We never came home empty handed! This was a normal family activity. I haven't been able to pass on the enthusiasm for this activity to... anyone.

Not only did I enjoy learning to grow things, but I loved selling them too. I sold my first pumpkin when I was five years old at the old Food-Town where Beaver Street Brewery is now located. At seven, an elderly friend asked if I would pick a bouquet of sweet peas, thinking I would enjoy their soft colors and pleasing fragrance. Returning home, I promptly divided them up and was out selling them to the neighbors. When I was twelve, I learned to transplant aspens and was giving them away up and down the street.

This book is a compilation of all I have learned over sixty years of gardening in Flagstaff. I don't have a horticultural degree. I've never taken the Master Gardening class, although I would like to. I have taught classes and done yard tours. The years I have had money for the class I didn't have time, and the years I have time, I haven't had the money. This is practical, hands-on advice that I hope is helpful. When we struggle with difficult economic times, this is the knowledge passed down from an older generation, calling to mind a time when we all moved a bit slower and enjoyed the pleasure of digging in the earth, and picking the 'fruit of our labors'. Happy gardening!

CHAPTER 1: CATCHING A VISION

During World War II, food was rationed; labor and transportation were diverted to support our troops. This created a shortage of fresh vegetables for many Americans. The United States government encouraged people to plant "Victory Gardens" so they could provide their own fruits and vegetables, leaving canned goods to be used for the men and women of our Armed Forces. Twenty million Americans signed up and planted gardens in front yards, in empty lots and on rooftops. Neighbors formed cooperatives; some would grow one thing, others something else. In 1943, 9-10 million tons of produce was grown by suburban America, equaling the commercial output raised on farms! Unfortunately, as soon as the war ended, tract homes became the status quo. The Victory Gardens died out and boring lawns replaced plots of tomatoes, squash and beans. Now after sixty years of lying dormant, the sustainable garden is making a comeback! The front yard is not reserved for just lawn and flowers anymore.

In the late summer of 1999, I had a life-changing event take place. My church family, Flagstaff Christian Fellowship, was hosting six men from around the world. Three were from Asia, Nepal, Pakistan and South Korea. The other three from Africa: Nigeria, Sierra Leone and Liberia. The men were speaking during the week but time had been reserved to show them the great wonders in Northern Arizona. The day we went to the Grand Canyon we stopped by my house in Cheshire. We ended up standing in my driveway chatting while waiting for another person to arrive.

The men had been talking and one called me over to ask a question, "Julie, why do all of these houses have grass in their front yards? Why aren't people growing things they can eat?" The six men looked at me waiting for me to give a rational explanation for what seemed to them incredulously ridiculous. I lamely answered, "It's just what we do." As we drove away I looked at my own yard, my neighborhood and eventually my city in a whole different way. Why aren't we growing food in our front yards?

There seems to be some sort of unwritten rule stating that all front yards should look similar, one or two trees, a stretch of lawn, maybe some shrubs with a little river rock for contrast. We see our lots as small, believing not much could be done with them. We fall into the trap of monotony, failing to think beyond our limited vision. If we have a vegetable garden, it should be properly in its place in the corner of the BACKYARD. Let's challenge our thinking and learn from our international friends. There are so many options. Let's build something both beautiful and edible on our properties.

Imagine What You Can Do With Your Property

One of the best pieces of advice I have received was to grow what you want to grow. Sounds simple but often we don't do it.

Biologist, Peter Price from the United Kingdom, lives down my street. His garden is different from any yard in our neighborhood. He has packed every inch of space with plants, leaving just a tiny portion for a patch of grass. He has more in his yard than ten yards combined. My neighbor next door converted his yard to all native plants and trees.

Another friend has a vegetable garden on a busy street in front of his business. He asked if I could harvest for him while he went on vacation. I had so many people stopping to admire the lush beds and ask questions, I could barely get the harvesting done. Another home in the older section of town has a Victorian garden, complete with gates and arbors displaying the plants and flowers that were popular during that era. As in many communities, Flagstaff is seeing a resurgence of community gardens with open space being leased to those without their own lots.

Ask yourself, "What do I like? What do I want my yard to look like?" Even if your living arrangements are temporary, you can move plants, give them away or leave them for the next owners. Take a walk around your property and think about what you have to work with. Remember to consider porches, driveways, balconies, roofs, and walls for vertical plants, steps, fences, alleys and easements. Each of these elements offers opportunity to think beyond a strip of grass.

Sometimes a lawn is the best way to go. When my four kids were small, the yard was all lawn with a narrow strip for a flower bed. The lawn served as the neighborhood football field, the best use at the time. My toddlers spent happy hours in a sandbox. The sand is now a great addition to my current garden. As my kids grew and I had more time, I began to expand the flower beds until they were across the front of the house. After the conversation with my international friends, I began to speculate about how to use the bottom of the front yard, street-side. I thought about how well squash plants would do in full sun. I decided to try it. I started with four squash plants. I was a little nervous because it seemed like a radical idea. I had NEVER seen vegetables planted in front yards and wasn't sure how people would respond to seeing squash growing in the front yard. Not a single negative comment, yet! I notice more and more vegetables popping up in front yards throughout the neighborhood each year. I noticed a couple of years ago an expensive home had pole beans climbing up a trellis on the front porch. The vines of pumpkins ramble along green lawns. It's just a matter of time until rows of corn stretch up to the sky. People are feeling more comfortable being creative and expressing themselves through gardening. Every year I see more and more front yard gardens. I continue to be amazed at the creativity and beauty!

There are many advantages to having vegetables in your front yard. Here are a few:

1. They are pretty! The leaves, flowers, and textures add variety and beauty to the existing landscape. Giant rhubarb leaves, brightly colored chard, climbing beans, squash blossoms and pumpkins sprawling out across a driveway, down a slope or into the neighbor's yard get rave reviews. When it comes to passing comments, flowers take a back seat to the veggies.

2. There is usually more sun. The street and driveway guarantee an open space without shade from trees or buildings.

3. Veggies like lots of manure. It's easier to put it in the front yard than to haul it around to the back yard.

4. It's a guaranteed conversation starter! A great way to get to know your neighbors and meet new people is to be out planting, weeding, and picking. If you're not a people person, don't plant vegetables in your front yard.

One word of caution: start small. You can come up with a master plan or have vision that may take ten years to implement. Don't try to do it all in one year. I know so many people who start out enthusiastically and try to take on too much. They find out that watering, weeding and harvesting takes too much time. Some spread out good soil instead of concentrating it in one place. Plants will become feeble and produce anemic fruit. Better to start small and expand each year rather than burning out over a miserable experience with no desire to ever see a trowel again!

CHAPTER 2: UNDERSTANDING YOUR MICROCLIMATE

For some areas of the country, microclimate is not as serious a consideration as in Flagstaff, Arizona. If you live in an area where there is high humidity, little wind and relatively flat ground, microclimate has little bearing. BUT if you live in Flagstaff or a similar dry, windy, mountainous area, consideration of the microclimate within your yard is essential in creating a successful garden.

In Flagstaff, we have more varied microclimates than some entire regions in other parts of the country! We have the "banana belt" at the foot of Mount Elden. The neighborhoods within the "banana belt" such as Swiss Manor and Upper Greenlaw have 150 days of a growing season! Not ten miles, as the crow flies, we have the "arctic" of Flagstaff, Baderville. It sits in an open meadow at the base of the San Francisco Peaks with a growing season of thirty days. Neighborhoods throughout Flagstaff present a wide range between the two extremes. I refer to my own neighborhood, Cheshire, just four miles from Baderville as the "Siberia" of Flagstaff. Cheshire is not as extreme as Baderville but still COLD. I'm afraid to find out the technical length of our growing season!

Within Cheshire there are microclimates. I live along the Rio de Flag, which is the lowest point in Cheshire. The cold air creeps off the nearby San Francisco Peaks, sinking along the creek bed, haunting backyard gardens. My home is colder than the neighbor's home across the street. On a summer evening walk, you will feel the difference in air temperature just passing by the Rio.

On each and every lot, there are microclimates. Depending on the direction your house faces, the exposure at different times of the year, land features, trees, fences and out buildings, all come into play in considering the microclimates within your lot. Each variety of plants has slightly different requirements. Applying what you learn about your microclimates will enable you to match the right plant with the right location within your own yard.

First, determine the general microclimate of your neighborhood. Knowing two things will help with this. Warm air rises and cold air sinks. If you are in a valley, you will be colder than your neighbors on a hill. I have friends whose yard is sloped and there is a huge difference between their back-property line at the bottom of the hill and the top of their yard. Begin to ask questions of your neighbors, especially those that garden and have been in their homes awhile. Make use of the county home extension office as well.

Observation is Effective

There is nothing like thoroughly studying your yard to get the most accurate information. Draw a map of your home. Mark the sunny, warm areas on your map. Sometimes this will be obvious as you recall where the snow melts first, where the dog sleeps on a chilly day or what area dries out first.

On a day when you will be home, go out every hour and see where the direct sunlight falls and mark that on your map. It may take several days to do this. This is best done in April or May, August or September to get an overall idea of exposure. The areas receiving direct sunlight in January may not be in direct sun during the growing season, but knowing the location of the winter sunlight is valuable in planting perennial beds.

Accurately assessing your yard is important, as it is so easy to be deceived believing an area gets lots of sun. Your potential garden site may look very sunny on your way to work and when you get home, but it was in the shade most of the day. Your prime locations are going to be where you get good morning sun that lasts until at least 1:00 or 2:00 in the afternoon.

Secure your best areas for your most demanding plants, usually in the vegetable family including tomatoes, cucumbers, basil, and squash. Due to living in Flagstaff's version of Siberia, I place my tomatoes next to the house. They only get sun during the morning, but they get protection from the wind.

The squash family will not tolerate diminished sun, demanding as much as possible to do well. They will do better when out in the open in a sunny spot, which is why I place them in the front yard.

The north side may not get as much sun, but many perennials love the cool protection and moisture this exposure provides. As a rule, vegetables will not do well in the shade provided by the house, so plant flowers in beds close to the structure. The southern exposure is great for lots of things, including perennials, all bulbs and perennial vegetables like asparagus and rhubarb. As the zenith of the sun is very high in the summer, the southern exposure of some homes may not get as much sun in the summer. If this is your observation, the southern exposure may be a good area for any leafy vegetables, beans and root crops. The western exposure is the most difficult. It takes the hard west winds with the sun arriving mid-afternoon. I plant lots of bulbs in this area along with my most hardy perennials. I have a beautiful area under my back living room window that I really enjoy from spring to fall but this remains the domain of all the "tough" guys in my garden.

Creating Miniature Microclimate

Each area of your yard can be enhanced by the use of rocks, pots or stepping-stones. In my perennial beds, I use lots of stepping stones, mostly sandstone, with a few, flat, malapais rocks. These make it easy for me to move throughout the bed to pick flowers, weeds, transplant or simply enjoy the plants. Along with providing run-off, the rock retains moisture beneath it for the neighboring plants. I've added some large rocks for interest while creating microclimates within each patch of garden. The rock provides heat and protection on the south and east sides. The north side stays cool, moist and shady. The use of black pots or black plastic mulch can increase heat.

Start now by observing, and remember that understanding the minuscule variations throughout your yard takes time. Two years ago, I thought I could plant some things along the sidewalk. My perception was that this strip got a good amount of sun. I planted a twenty-foot row of beans on an area I had recently covered with cardboard and a few inches of manure. Much to my surprise, half of the bed lagged two weeks behind in coming up and barely produced a crop. I didn't realize that the end of the row received a lot of shade from a large white fir during the day. That area now has daffodils and columbine. Observe, experiment, and remember!

Transforming the Ditch

Growing up in the Coconino Estates subdivision I had a great time exploring the ditch that ran behind our home. A small creek ran in the spring when there was enough snowmelt. On years with rapid snow melt, the creek sometimes flooded all of downtown Flagstaff before passing on to the Little Colorado River. It was a great place to play and have adventures. When we moved to Cheshire in 1977, we intentionally picked a lot that bordered the ditch, near the headwaters of the Rio de Flag.

The contractor who built the homes was required by law to fence the entire length of the ditch because of safety. I discovered the section behind my house was much more active than it appeared to be a few miles south. Springs are abundant in Cheshire and the dam built by homesteaders 100 years ago keeps most of the runoff from flowing any further. A couple of years after we moved in, I persuaded my husband to put a gate in the fence. The possibilities now bloomed in front of me! When I stepped outside that gate, I might as well have been in a different world. I could do anything back there. After checking with the city and getting permission, I started planting trees. My neighbor, Tom Whitham, a research biologist at Northern Arizona University (NAU), planted many trees for his research as well. I had a vision for a beautiful place, but when I led, or should I say dragged, friends and family out to see it all they saw were weeds and baby trees no taller than the sticks which were supporting them. Today, forty years later, it is just as beautiful as I knew it would be. Thousands of spring bulbs and perennial flowers are scattered along it. Vegetable beds filled with the vines of winter squash, gourds and pumpkins spread along the banks. The feathery fronds of asparagus rise along the other plants while vines of sugar snap peas climb the fence. Fifty trees provide a shady arbor for both birds and people. In addition to being a beautiful spot in the ditch, the Audubon Society did a bird count in Flagstaff, and found the largest variety of species in the mini-ecosystem behind our house!

The trees and shrubs also changed the microclimate and growing conditions along the ditch. The channel being the lowest point in Cheshire has some brutal frosts. The trees act as a protective cover and windbreak now, which has extended its growing season by several weeks. Cold air flows along the channel just like a river but when it hits the trees it's now diverted. The trees have created a more humid environment, helping other vegetation to grow better. On a hot summer day, the ditch is usually teaming with grasshoppers and very warm with the direct sunlight. When you walk under the section with the trees, the air is obviously cooler and more humid. It's also grasshopper-free because they don't like the humidity or shade. There is a trail that runs along the ditch. Many people walk or ride their bikes along it. I still love going out there, but now see just as many people back there, as there are in the street out front.

One other thing has changed- I used to drag people back there to see its potential but now they are asking me for a tour of the ditch!

The ditch behind my house: BEFORE

The ditch: AFTER

CHAPTER 3: CONVERTING YOUR LAWN TO GARDEN

Buying this book was worth the price for this chapter alone! This single tip (for the life of me I can't remember where I got it!) has saved me hundreds of hours and a boatload of frustration. NEVER try to remove grass by digging up the sod with a shovel or rototiller. Manual removal is next to impossible because any roots left behind will soon sprout above the surface and spread again. Grass by its very nature, provides multiple nutrients to the soil. The green blades, brown thatch and thick roots are filled with nutrients, which you really want to save in the soil.

The Cardboard Method

Decide on an area where you want a garden instead of lawn. This also works for eliminating clover, weeds, or other ground covers you want to get rid of. You may do this at any time of the year. Break down cardboard boxes and lay them flat. Overlap the edges across the area you want to transform. One layer will work but two is better. Use several layers of newspaper over gaps in the cardboard or to round square edges. MAKE SURE NO GRASS IS LEFT EXPOSED. Check carefully along your edges; near sidewalks, paths and driveways. Place a few rocks on top of the cardboard to hold it in place. The rocks are temporary. Now cover the cardboard with some type of organic matter. Leaves are great in the fall; grass clippings will work in the spring or summer. A truckload of manure can't be beat. You can use compost or garden dirt. Or a combination of these. This is easiest on a non-windy day. The cardboard should be completely covered.

It is possible to do some planting as soon as this is done. Put a layer of soil at least an inch on top of your choice of organic material. You can plant annual veggies or flowers as long as they don't have a deep root. I have found that a wildflower mix is lovely, cosmos and nasturtiums work well too. For vegetables, beans or lettuce are a good choice. It is important that the cardboard layer stays intact.

Here is another suggestion and fun thing to try. You can build up a few mounds of soil about 8 inches deep on top of your organic material. Plants like pumpkins, winter squash or gourds require the deeper soil to grow. The vines will grow rapidly and cover the area in no time.

The cardboard method takes a full year to complete before you can dig into the top layers. It is important to leave the cardboard intact.

Do not rush it- wait for full decomposition. After a year, turn everything over with a spade. The cardboard should be completely decomposed. Remove any leftover packing tape or other trash. The grass will be dead, decomposed into the soil, leaving all of the nutrients. Now use the bed for anything you want- vegetables, bulbs, perennials, etc.

Over a five-year span I converted half of my lawn into a garden and it was nearly effortless! The biggest challenge was finding sufficient organic material to cover the cardboard. As I noted previously, this method takes much of the more strenuous labor out of converting your lawn into a functional garden.

CHAPTER 4: COMPOSTING

Decomposition is a natural occurrence, as life forms break down and return to organic material. I once had someone rush up to me in distress saying, "I think I did something wrong with my compost!" Compost will happen. All we are doing with a compost bin is speeding up the process.

Why is Compost so Important?

Compost is vital in Flagstaff and other parts of the southwest because we don't have soil here, just various forms of rock and clay. The rocks; malapais, sandstone, limestone and cinders- none of them are favorable for growing plants. Compost is much more than amending the soil; it is almost creating the soil. Like the saying, "you are what you eat", the same is true for plants. They need a loose, healthy soil for roots to grow easily and provide needed nutrition.

A wildflower mix growing on top of a compost pile.

There are generally two problems that plagues compost. The mix is either too dry or too wet. The compost pile needs to be moist, not saturated. If it is too dry, try soaking some of your ingredients in water and mixing them into the pile. If the compost is soggy, try mixing shredded newspaper into the pile.

Here are two different ways to compost and I recommend practicing both forms:

Active Composting

When speaking of compost, most people refer to a bin of some sort for yard waste and kitchen scraps. Keep in mind that compost needs three square feet to internally heat the pile, maximizing decomposition. However, you can use something smaller. To make a quick, easy bin, cut off the bottom of an old plastic garbage can and turn the can upside down with the largest circumference on the ground. I cover the top with an old air mattress, preferably a dark color to draw heat, but any non-permeable material will do. Covering the can allows you to control the amount of moisture in the compost. Compost that is too dry tends to be a problem in the arid southwest so add water as needed.

Using a container like a garbage can, keeps the household waste confined and the animals out. We'll call this your main compost bin. DO NOT add meat or dairy to the compost bin.

When you wish to aerate your compost, tip the container over. Then use a garden fork to turn the compost. A shovel will work, though it may compact the pile. My preference is to use my hands, with rubber gloves of course! Mixing, stirring, adding new ingredients. It's the closest I get to baking.

The more frequently you turn the compost, the faster it will decompose. Turning adds oxygen while mixing the dry and moist ingredients. You can let it go for months without disruption. I don't turn the compost at all during summer, I'm too busy in the garden! As I've planted close to the bins, I don't want to risk tipping over the bin and crushing the plants.

In June, I usually plant seeds in the top of the composting bin. Beans are perfect. They grow wonderfully in the compost, producing lots of beans and adding nitrogen to the soil. Their roots, in turn, help to break down the compost. The bean plants are a reminder to add water as it would be easy to let the compost dry out. At the end of the summer, the level of compost within the bin has shrunk down about a foot and it's perfect, ready for the next season. I lift the bin off the finished compost and move the container to another part of the garden. Whether I move the compost or the bin, I am starting with an empty bin again.

Passive Composting

If you have access to large amounts of yard waste, a second pile for passive compost is a good idea. This means an area where you pile leaves, garden debris and weeds for months at a time. A couple of years ago I was walking behind my house along the ditch where I have a large garden bed. I noticed a zucchini plant doing very poorly despite great exposure and plenty of water. As I examined the plant, I realized that the soil in that bed had not been amended for about ten years. That fall I began piling all the weeds I pulled in a pile where that zucchini had been. Over the next spring and summer I added more weeds. Last year, I planted directly on the pile and had the most beautiful, healthy zucchini imaginable! A loose pile of weeds and leaves sounds unsightly, but it actually blends into the garden-look. The pile is constantly decomposing underneath the top layer so it never gets very high.

If the weeds have begun to go to seed, most of the seeds are deep in the pile. If they germinate they will die out for lack of sunshine. Any seeds close to the surface that might sprout are confined in a small area and can quickly be removed.

One of my favorite ingredients for compost are bags of leaves set out for bulky trash. I keep an eye out for homes with good trees; aspen or maple are my favorite. No matter how hard I have tried to speed up the leaves' composting process in the fall, they are never ready by spring. Adding coffee grounds, manure, and kitchen waste, help- but alas, the leaves are not "finished". Here's my solution. I use a couple of bins of partially decomposed leaves and pack them into large black plastic pots strategically placed to act as a "hose guard" so I don't flatten plants while moving the hose around the yard. Just like in a compost bin, place a couple of inches of soil on top, sprinkle bean seeds liberally, add another inch of soil. The beans look beautiful, you get a bumper crop AND by September I have perfectly finished compost.

When starting your passive compost, mix the coffee grounds with the leaves. Don't leave them in a clump (T&E)*. Adding moist garden dirt and manure into the leaves helps contribute the necessary organisms to get the compost going.

Avid gardeners come to love compost and soon find they cannot generate enough to supply all of the needs. An excellent option is to get manure from a local source. Avoid manure that has been mixed with sawdust (T&E). Sawdust breaks down very slowly, robbing the soil of nitrogen in the process. Manure mixed with straw is a good combination. IF a stable is not an option, purchase the CHEAPEST steer manure from a store.

Starbucks (and other coffee shops too) has a bucket set out that says "Grounds for your garden". Help yourself! If you don't see the bucket, ask! Be sure to ask for the espresso pods too. The grounds sometimes are put back in the foil bags they originated from but often leak. Keep a container in your car to haul them away mess-free (T&E).

T&E stands for "Trial and Error". These are things I have learned the hard way. Without going into all of the gruesome, embarrassing or boring details- take my word for it!

Worm Composting

In the first edition of this book I described the joys and benefits of worm composting. That was before I suffered through several worm tragedies. Even with my low standards I found I did not like keeping a worm compost bin in the house or the garage. I moved them outside but in my effort to keep the red wigglers separate and genetically pure for sales purposes, I put them in old trash cans. The cans retained too much moisture and some worms drowned. The cans also got too cold and many froze. I felt so bad, I put the survivors in the general compost where they are currently thriving. I cannot guarantee they are all genetically pure red wigglers but sales of "worm mutts" are good!

> **ABOUT RED WIGGLERS:**
> Red wigglers (Eisenia fetida) need to be fed. Kitchen scraps, leaves and manure will keep them happy. Red wigglers are only to be used in compost, they should not to be put in the garden soil.

Compost Ingredients

Kitchen Waste:
Veggie scraps raw or
        cooked
Fruit
Coffee grounds
Tea and tea bags
Espresso
Breads, pasta
Cereals, including
leftovers with milk
Grains
Rice
Leftovers without
meat (casseroles)
Eggshells
Shrimp shells

Paper Products:
Newspaper
Shredded paper
Paper towels
Cardboard

Sweets & Treats:
Flour/sugar
Cake
Cookies
Pastries
Candies

Yard Waste:
Vegetable clippings
Flower clippings
Grass clippings
Leaves
Weeds
Plants
Garden dirt, add a
shovel full frequently
to add the necessary
organisms

Manure:
Grain-fed animals
and their bedding
(horses, cows, goats,
sheep)
Elk

(Manure cont.)
Chickens and other
birds
Rabbit

Beverages:
Fruit juice
Gatorade
Coffee, tea
Soda
Alcohol

Limit:
Dairy
Citrus
Onions
Sawdust
Pine needles

NO! NO! NEVER!
Meats
Fat
Cat or dog waste
Rose stems (T&E)

CHAPTER 5: PREPARING THE SOIL AND PLANTING YOUR GARDEN

Get ready, set, go! The garden really begins in December. My favorite day is in late December, usually it's snowing and blowing when I open my mailbox and there it is! My first seed catalog! What a delight to see those bright, colorful pictures of beautiful flowers and wonderful vegetables. Outside, the earth is white with snow, or brown, everything looking dead. Inside, I turn pages of garden magazines and dream of the next season.

The time to order is as soon as possible. There are many advantages to ordering early. With our short growing season in Flagstaff, some veggies and flowers need to be started in January. You get a jump on supply because seed catalogs often run out of certain varieties. The ordering process gets you thinking about and planning your garden.

Compare the same items in different catalogs because there can be big differences. Order the larger quantities and you will be amazed at the price savings. I try to buy enough to last five to seven years. Winter is also the time to get your order in for seed potatoes and onion sets, asparagus and rhubarb. They may send them at a later date, but you can prepare the ground before the actual stock arrives.

Sharing an order with a few garden friends is fun and allows you to order larger quantities and save more money. The bigger the order, the more you save, and sharing helps reduce shipping costs. Learn also to read between the lines of the gardening lingo: "vigorous" means it is going to take over, "compact" means that is has been hybridized to accommodate a small garden and probably won't produce much. If you have questions, call customer service.

Preparing the Soil

Soil preparation really goes on year-round. As you move forward with composting, you will have several bins, each at a different stage of decomposition. If you are converting lawn to garden, that will be in progress as well. Yet the most work occurs in the spring; turning the soil. If possible, get out and start in early spring, February or even March if the soil is not too saturated or frozen. If your soil is dry or compacted, soak it to make it easier to turn. Soak the ground a couple of days before you want to turn it.

Turning the soil benefits the garden in several ways. First, turning the soil exposes eggs or larvae of insects to frost, thereby killing them. The thought of gaining a jump on grasshopper destruction is worth getting out there!

You also get a jump on weeds that have made an early appearance. Every once in a while, you will find a plant that has volunteered in the garden area that you will want to transplant.

Turning the dirt aerates (adds oxygen to) the soil while giving us some great exercise. Since turning the soil is hard work, it is not unpleasant to do this chore on a chilly day. Doing a quick turn in the spring makes it much easier when you turn the soil again before planting. You can add compost or manure during the first turn or wait until planting. Keep a bucket nearby to toss in rocks that come to the surface.

Early planting begins in March or April, and that comes surprisingly fast. As the weather warms up and you anticipate planting seeds and seedlings, rake your garden beds fairly flat. Some vegetables prefer to be planted on a small mound, so begin shaping these in preparation for planting.

I always plant more closely than the seed packages recommend. The emerging plants seem to do just fine and this greatly increases the yield. I'm not sure who the suggested distance is written for, but surely for someone who has a lot more land to work with than I do. I also have given up planting in rows. As I looked at my lettuce one year, I thought, "I'm doing this the wrong way! Look at all the wasted space, why don't I just scatter the seeds around in this whole area and use every bit of space?" I've been doing that ever since and it has worked great. If the area is big enough, I place a few stepping stones so I can get around easily to water, weed and harvest. I would recommend this with any type of lettuce, chard, spinach, beets, carrots, beans, kale, almost all herbs, annual flowers like cosmos, zinnias and marigolds.

I find it almost impossible to toss out seedlings that have been thinned so I end up moving them somewhere else. As long as the root is intact they usually do great! Be sure to trim the seedlings so they don't have so many green leaves to support until the roots system is established. Once, when I was harvesting a garden for a friend, I found that someone else had come earlier in the day and thinned the chard. It was lying helpless, in a heap. I took the chard home, trimmed the outer leaves and ate them. I soaked the plants overnight, and then planted about 60 chard in every nook and cranny I could find in my yard. Every single plant survived, grew, produced and came up the next spring.

When actually planting the seed, remember that the bigger the seed, the deeper it goes. This is a helpful rule of thumb. Because of our dry climate, it is better to err on the side of planting a bit too deep than too shallow. Seed that dries out will not sprout. Also, the smaller the seed, the more shallow it is planted, the more you need to sprinkle it till it germinates. Larger seeds can get one good watering every few days and be fine.

Planting the Seed

Remember to soak a good number of seeds (including peas, the squash family, and chard) to help ensure germination. You will not see this on the seed packet or read about it in most garden magazines or books. Most gardeners across the U.S. are fighting fungus and rot. They wouldn't dream of soaking seeds! Soaking the seeds makes a huge difference in our dry climate. The arid soil can cause seeds to dry out, never getting moist enough to germinate.

Lay out your garden in the way you'd like it, considering what works best for you and what is best for the plants. I find I use fewer rows. I am doing more "sprinkling" of seeds, then covering with a layer of fine soil seems to be the best use of limited space.

Place peas along a fence where they can climb the links. I plant my lettuce next to the peas. They are both spring crops so it makes it easy to water them at the same time.

Squash are scattered throughout the garden where they will thrive in the sunny, rich soil. I often place them in groups or along curving trails. Pole beans are planted where they can climb while bush beans sprout from large pots. These pots are usually filled to the top, the bean seeds are planted very close together. This is an ideal way to raise beans. They stay clean, free from insects, are easy to pick, and the leaves in the compost are completely decomposed by the end of the summer. These pots are located strategically, acting as a "hose guard" to keep me from running over plants as I pull the hose through the garden.

Soak the soil thoroughly after planting. The larger the seed, the less it needs water after planting. For example, after giving beans or soaked peas a good watering, wait several days to water again. Waiting may actually help them to germinate, as wet soil stays cool. You want the soil to warm up for good germination. Tiny seeds, like lettuce and some flowers, are planted very shallow. These dry out quickly and need to be sprinkled once a day if possible.

Planting in Containers

Almost everything you can grow in the garden, you can grow in a container. That is good news if you have a small area. As discussed in the chapter on vegetables, all my tomatoes are grown in black pots. I also have two metal water troughs with holes for drainage. I used these for lettuce, but they would be great for herbs, flowers or beans. Squash, beans, lettuce, chard, peas, herbs, flowers of all kinds, can be grown in containers, some even do better in a container! In choosing the size of the container, remember how large the plant will be when it matures and the amount of space the roots will require.

Lettuce growing in an animal trough found in bulky trash.

Perennials should not be left over the winter in a pot outside. It is very hard on them over the winter as the pot continually gets warm then very cold. It is also difficult to keep the plant watered.

Three important things about container growing:

1.   Make sure the pot is adequate for what you are potting. For vegetables I like to use a pot at least 18 inches deep.

2.   For a growing medium, combine a really good soil, potting mix, and compost. You will probably need to use some sort of fertilizer to provide adequate nutrition in the confined pot.

3.   You must water every day! This is essential. A pot dries out so quickly, much faster than plants in the ground. Watering everything in pots needs to be part of your daily schedule.

So we've talked about preparing the soil. In the spring, you've worked in the manure and other compost elements. You may have even tenderly tucked the seeds and seedlings into the soil. Now consider…

Being Prepared is Everything in a Mountain Garden

The calendar says today is May 21st. As I write this, we are preparing for a major cold front to pass through Flagstaff. Temperatures are predicted to drop to freezing. As this is almost an annual event in the Southwest, it is good to know how to deal with "cold snaps" so that you don't lose everything you have worked for in the last few weeks.

These events are not usually confined to one cold night. They begin with the wind, sometimes lasting for several days. The front may bring precipitation in the form of rain, hail, snow, or sleet. This is followed by cold air with at least one or two nights of below freezing temperatures. We were all sure spring had arrived but the temperature outside feels more like winter.

This is pure misery for plants. In my experience, the cold weather crops such as lettuce, chard, peas, and root crops will be fine through the cold snap. They might appreciate a layer of hay to protect them if it doesn't blow away. Some kind of shelter, such as a lawn chair or chaise lounge placed carefully over the lettuce will protect it from damage. A rock placed on the lawn chairs will help anchor them if it's windy.

Bring any tender annual or vegetables growing in pots into the garage or house. Outside, your most sensitive plants are the squash family, peppers, cucumbers, beans and tomatoes. The key (T&E) is to cover the tender seedlings in the beginning and leave them covered for the duration of the passing cold front. For years, I spent many hours covering my garden at night then uncovering it during the day… why? The plants will be blasted by the wind, hailed on, frozen back for the season! This may last for a week! You'll discover in leaving the cover in place that the plants will be fine, and you will save yourself a TON of work.

In 2010, we suffered through three weeks of cold temperatures. Each day seemed as if summer would never arrive. I had my garden ready to go with many of the squash plants already in the ground, expecting the season to progress as normal. Earlier I had recovered several large clear plastic containers from the trash.

I knew that plastic alone would not help. The plastic pulls in the cold air, making the inside even colder than the outside. I thought if

Squash enjoying "greenhouse" life.

I added a one-gallon plastic milk jug filled with water that might offset the cold temperatures at night by using passive solar heat. The water absorbs the heat during the day, then releases it at night as the temperatures drop. I did not remove the plastic during the entire three-week period.

What a reward! The growth of the plants over the next month exploded unlike I had experienced previously. Each plant loved its own little greenhouse. I had squash on each plant by early July.

The jugs also work well alone. I place one next to each tomato plant inside its cage. It's a tight fit! I plant winter squash later, in May, but a jug next to each plant will help them as well.

Two to five gallon water containers also work well. Especially for plants that grow taller. I have used them on summer squash, in a tunnel, winter squash and pumpkins, and peppers.

Remember for all plants you want to protect the "guts" of the plant, don't worry about outer leaves. If you don't have the large, clear, plastic containers, place some hay, dry leaves, newspaper, shredded paper, or cloth to protect the inner circle of the plant. With really cold weather, add a light sheet. You can cover several plants with one sheet. Do this before the wind is blowing fifty miles an hour- much easier! This arrangement will protect down to about twenty degrees. If one night is especially cold, add a light blanket on top of the sheet.

If your area is expecting only a light frost, or even the potential of frost, there is nothing better than a laundry basket (T&E). It protects while letting air circulate. Avoid anything that touches the leaves directly.

You know that tomatoes are very tender so be well prepared with sheets every night until temperatures stabilize in the lower 40's. Place hay or newspaper around the stem. Using clothespins, "swaddle" all the plants by securing the sheet to the cages wires. Make sure you have the ends covered. You may need to use a rock or lean something up against the sheet to hold it into place. Use another sheet on top if it is going to be extra cold.

Using these precautions, your plants will be fine for the duration if you leave them covered. Generally, you don't need to water them. Watering tends to make the air colder (hypothermia) and increase the chances of freezing. However, if the soil dries out, watering may become necessary.

As I mentioned in the section on beans, they are so difficult to cover, and have such a short growing season I like to plant in mid-June, avoiding the cold snaps. Germination is seven to ten days. Plant beans during a warm spell, 75* or above. They germinate much better.

Pole beans do need to go in earlier, mid-May, but the pole can be helpful in providing a "prop" to protect them. Hay, with a sheet tied and draped from the pole usually is adequate protection.

Other ideas for protection (when you get really desperate):

- Cardboard boxes secured with a rock
- Ladder, with a sheet over it
- Card table
- Board supported on two, five-gallon buckets covered with a sheet and secured with a rock. This could protect up to 10 feet or more.
- Any lawn furniture or tables

Water Conservation

Water conservation is a huge issue to all of the inter-mountain west. Using water wisely may not have been a problem for you in the past, it could be in the future. Wise water use is important for everyone to learn in conserving a natural resource. Knowing the water requirements for different plants will help you in determining your water schedule and use. Dry years or drought can cause water shortages and rationing. You may have a family emergency, which calls you away from home for several weeks. Knowing which plants to help first is invaluable. This is "Water Triage 101".

When considering what is most critical to water, the first priority goes to anything growing in a pot. They dry out quickly and can't go for more than a few days without water. The next priority would be annuals, including both flowers and vegetables. They become even needier if they are blooming or producing fruit.

Perennials are extremely hardy, and a good, deep, watering will last for weeks. They may be stressed, but they will survive, especially if they are more than one-year-old. Here is a great tip on grass: grass that is well established will simply go dormant if it does not receive water. You can let it go! As soon as the rains come, or you get around to watering, the grass ends its dormant state.

Here are some more tips for using water wisely:

- Infrequent, deep, watering for established plants is much better than a frequent sprinkle

- Put gutters around your home and collect rainwater. You don't have to have a fancy rain barrel, you can use a garbage can to collect the runoff. A screen over the top or lid when not in use keeps mosquitoes or other insects and birds out. I am always rescuing ladybugs that have fallen in!

- Plant water loving plants near the water barrels. I have rhubarb near three of mine. They get loads of water that way.

- The more water you use, the more you pay per gallon so all conservation measures payoff.

- You will often read in garden literature not to water in the evening because of mold, fungus, etc. This is directed at the more humid states and does not apply to arid climates. I would say water in the evening, especially in hot dry months. This allows the plant to soak in the water all night long. You greatly minimize evaporation that would be lost in our dry, windy, and sunny days.

- I always take my dish water out to my flowers. Contrary to popular belief, plants appreciate the phosphate in dish soap!

- Think WATER when you shovel the snow! I intentionally shovel some areas to give plants extra moisture in the spring.

- Rocks and stepping-stones increase water to all the plants around them.

- Mulch and bark help retain water. However, wait to add the mulch till your plants are firmly established. Adding mulch to garden beds before the seedlings are established may cool off the soil and keep them from making an appearance. Mulch will also help control the weeds and save some labor.

- Manure and compost help to retain the water in the soil.
- I have to sleep with a hot water bottle, even in summer. The water never goes down the drain; it waters the geraniums on the front porch in summer or in winter, on the windowsill. Be creative with ways you can conserve water in your own home!
- Last, but not least, California's water saving slogan, "If it's yellow, let it mellow. If it's brown, flush it down."

Disclaimer: no matter how water conscious you are, every gardener needs the luxury of a nice HOT bath after a hard day of work in the garden!

CHAPTER 6: BEST PERENNIALS FOR THE MOUNTAINS OF THE SOUTHWEST

The terms "perennial" and "annual" cause lots of confusion among new growers. Here is an easy way to remember:

- Annuals are planted annually, every year.
- Perennials make our yards their homes.

When planning a garden bed, it is not a matter of choosing one or the other. Use both to create a lovely display. A perennial is like a friend who returns every year, bigger and better than the year before. Perennials are wonderful in so many ways! They grow in areas of the yard where annuals would struggle. They require very little care and are easier than a lawn! Although they appreciate good soil, many will tolerate a poorer soil unlike a vegetable or annual. If you plan correctly, you can have perennials in bloom from March- October.

These are some of my favorites:

New England Asters

I have not seen these in the nurseries but ordered them from a perennial catalog. Hot, and I do mean hot pink, light pink, blue, white, purple with a yellow center and a shade of magenta I cannot describe, all grace the flower beds of my yard and the ditch behind the house. These plants are very showy, extremely easy to care for, do well in sun or shade. Pinching back the branches may encourage the plant to become bushier. This tough plant does need a little care to get established but will bloom for years. Asters are not good for cutting and seem to have no fragrance. Bees love them!

New England Aster

Bleeding Heart

The first time I saw this lovely plant was while visiting my daughter at college in Iowa. As soon as I got home I bought it as a "memory plant". They are considered an heirloom plant as they can live for decades. They bloom very early in May, the stems arching upward with heart shaped flowers. They prefer deep shade and are a nice addition to the shade garden.

Bleeding Heart

Columbine

Everyone loves the Arizona Native Columbine! A hardy addition to any garden, columbine prefer the cooler, shaded areas of the yard. The plants spread by seed but are not truly invasive. Could you really have too many? I have had no success with the lovely blue Colorado columbine. A neighbor and I concluded that it is too dry here. I have also tried other members of the Aquila family in the various shades of reds, yellows and whites. They bloom but are outperformed by our native golden columbine.

A couple of years back, I noticed that some pest was stripping the leaves from the stems of the columbine. I took a close look and discovered tiny green worms on the underside of the leaves. I prefer to hand pick these pests, but a good insecticide will also finish them. Try to look for something that is natural, not toxic.

Columbine

Coneflower family

Any and all flowers in this family are wonderful. From the purple and white Echinacea to the Black-Eyed Susan and Gloriosa Daisy this is a group that will give a great display. They flourish in either part shade or full sun with some varieties doing well in the challenging areas of the garden. They make a good, long lasting cut flower, although they lack fragrance.

Purple Coneflowers

Day Lilies

One of my favorite hybrid day lilies. Not knowing the technical name, I call it "Double Trouble" after my twin grandsons.

My family lived in the Coconino Estates area of Flagstaff when I was growing up, just three miles south of where I live now. When I was seven years old, I was walking along the Rio de Flag with some friends. We came upon some day lilies that someone had uprooted and tossed over their back fence. I didn't know what they were at the time. My friends continued their walk but I stopped and gathered them all up and took them home. I made a bed for them in the corner of the back yard, digging miniature canals around the plants to keep them well watered. Over the years, I have learned that this extra effort was completely unnecessary. Day lilies will grow without any help at all! From this original clump of Native American day lilies, this is not an exaggeration; there are now hundreds of thousands of day lilies around Flagstaff! You have to work to kill them.

Yet they are a wonderful, beautiful plant. The long narrow leaves come up very early in the spring with the edible flowers blooming on individual stocks the first week of July. The foliage looks good all the way through fall, turning a nice yellow. My original plants were the old heirloom lilies, which seem to be the hardiest, spreading the fastest. There are now whole catalogs devoted to day lilies, all sizes and descriptions with blooms of white, yellow, salmon, pink, wine, purple, red and bi-colors. While all the new varieties are not as hardy as the original, day lilies can afford diminished hardiness. The hybrids are great plants and a bit easier to manage. My Amish friend, Clara, has over 250 varieties and has been so generous in sharing them with me.

Daffodils

I LOVE daffodils! I love all spring bulbs but daffodils are definitely my favorite. This is partly because they do so well in Flagstaff. They love the change of season, the cold winters, even the snow. They are toxic, so they are safe from all our critters. The elk, deer and rabbits won't eat the leaves or flowers and the chipmunks nor squirrels will eat the bulbs. All animals instinctively avoid them. Daffodil bulbs can be planted in any exposure, in any type of soil, needing very little care. They do benefit greatly from a deep watering before and after they bloom. Plant each bulb 3 to 5 inches deep. Bone meal is recommended but I have had trouble

Daffodils

with dogs digging them up when they smelled the bone meal. The bulbs like sand, which is why they do so well in Holland. So if you have extra sand handy, maybe from a construction project or old sandbox, you can recycle it and mix some in the soil for them. Never cut the leaves as they are making food for the next year's blooms. They will naturally die back in June with the leaves disappearing. Daffodils are great by themselves or in the perennial bed. I mix them liberally with the perennials. I like to plant annuals near them as they begin to die back. This ensures that they continue to get water, the space they occupied will be filled with something pretty and I won't be tempted to dig in that spot, thinking I have an "opening" for a plant. I have run a shovel through more daffodil bulbs than I care to count. Good ideas for companion planting with daffodils are beans, nasturtiums, cosmos, chard, or lettuce.

There are over 2,300 varieties of daffodils, from miniatures to large flowered, double, bi and tri-colored or configurations that resemble a butterfly. All the colors are in the yellow, white and orange range, with a few pink and salmon colors. Some are even fragrant! They make a great cut flower but need to be placed in a vase by themselves, as they are also toxic to other flowers. I like to add a few dried pussy willow stems in the bouquets. Pussy willows come out about the same time in the spring. Do not be concerned about the toxicity to pets or children. None of them should have any desire to eat the daffodils either.

I also enjoy having crocus and grape hyacinths. Tulips are lovely but they are a tasty treat for critters and our dry air, wind and intense sun cause them too much grief.

Delphinium

Sometimes referred to as the queen of the garden, these are beautiful plants that are amazingly hardy. They do best against the house or fence because they grow so tall and, they need protection from strong winds and they may need to be staked. They do need care and attention. There are new colors now but the old blues are the hardiest.

Geraniums

My geraniums look lovely grouped and layered at the top of my driveway. One plant and all of the stands were found in the trash.

This might surprise you but I consider the geranium a perennial because my oldest is thirty years old. I always keep them in pots to make them easier to move. They spend their summers outdoors enjoying the beautiful weather and spend the winter inside blooming in a sun room. How can you beat that? A plant that blooms year-round, with an array of colors and leaf patterns and completely pest free! There are many new scented geraniums as well. They are easy to grow from seed or cuttings.

During the summer, I place the geraniums in a cluster at the top of the driveway. They get very little sun, but are completely happy there. Some go under the eaves of the house where they appreciate the protection from the wind and hard rains. They do not like to be out in full sun. A saucer under each plant ensures an adequate supply of water. A regular dose of Miracle Grow helps them to keep growing and blooming. At the end of the summer, before the first hard frost I cut them all back to about 4 inches. I do this because I am going to propagate them, but even if I didn't I would cut them back to about 6-8 inches to make them grow out nice and bushy and keep them from getting leggy. Geraniums can be trimmed back at any time. To propagate geraniums, use the oldest part of the stem, especially where there is a "V" in the stem, cut all the leaves off and place the 2-4 inch cutting in moist potting soil in a sunny window. Soon a new plant will sprout as roots develop on the cutting. I have about 80% success rate on the cuttings. With proper care geraniums can last for decades.

Hollyhocks

This story started thirty years ago with my neighbor, Peter Price, and masses of hollyhocks in his front yard. I had too many baby food jars that had been donated for a craft project. I thought, "I bet I could sell hollyhock seeds at the craft sale in the fall and use up all those baby food jars." So, with his permission I picked a ton of them, filled the baby food jars, and they did sell!

I gave one of the jars to my brother-in-law Dennis who had just bought a house in Camp Verde and had two acres to fill. He scattered them along a fence and in no time, they were everywhere. They were his pride and joy! Every year he would harvest

Standing with a friend's hollyhocks from seeds sold 10 years ago at the craft sale.

the hollyhock seeds and I would fill more jars. It's a contest every year to see if there will be more jars or more seeds!

A few years ago, I was talking to Peter, the original hollyhock source, and he told me the seeds came from an old homestead in Illinois. As a biologist, he was impressed with the variety of colors at this homestead. I was telling him how many jars we had sold over the years and he burst out laughing. "Well", he said, "that explains it! One of my friends was visiting from England and told me, 'There sure are a lot of hollyhocks in Flagstaff'!"

Hollyhocks are obviously easy to grow from seed. They don't bloom the first year but you will have them forever, cross-pollinating, treating gardeners to new and different colors. They need almost no care but will grow bigger with water and good soil. Sometimes I choose not to water them so they won't get so tall. A century ago little girls would play "wedding" with the flowers, using the white ones for the bride and colored ones for the wedding party. The open flowers were the skirts; the buds were the heads and bodice.

In 2017, I drove to Ouray, Colorado with my friend, Linda. Linda had lived in Ouray for 10 years, and she was going back to visit friends. I wanted to do research on my book, *Unbreakable Dolls of Colorado*. I got a cute room at a historic hotel downtown. I would go to the library or the local museum to do research. When I needed a break, I would take walks up and down the streets of Ouray. It was August and all the hollyhocks were in bloom. I thought they were so pretty and such a great variety of colors, too. I began harvesting seeds to take back to Flagstaff, thinking how these seeds would be a nice genetic addition to the seeds I was selling. When Linda picked me up, the first thing I said was, "Linda, look at all the beautiful hollyhocks! I don't remember seeing this many hollyhocks in Ouray before." Linda stopped the car, looked at me and said, "Julie, I bought hollyhock seeds at the craft sale every year and gave them to my friends in Ouray for Christmas."

Iris

Heriloom Iris

Irises are wonderful plants that have proven to be very easy to grow, offering lots of new and beautiful types and colors to experiment with in your garden. They are hardy and long lasting, willing to grow in almost any soil as long as they get a good amount of sun. They also multiply over time.

One big mistake to avoid is not to plant them too deep. The top third of the tuber MUST be exposed to the sun in order for them to bloom. It is torture to leave them exposed that way but force yourself to do it. Think of the rhizome as a turtle sunning itself in the sun. Irises seem to thrive on neglect and barely need to be watered. I have found that when you stray from the original iris colors of white, purple and yellow, the plants are not as hardy, multiply slower and bloom less. Beautiful as they are in the catalog, all the genetic engineering has its price!

Lenten Rose

A relatively new plant for me is the Hellebore, aka, Lenten Rose. It is an old heirloom plant from Europe and Asia, which has become very popular with the introduction of new colors and patterns in the flowers, which are both single and double.

Lenten Rose has quickly won my heart for a number of reasons. It is super hardy and does well here in Flagstaff. It can tolerate shade and is especially happy under a deciduous tree. It forms a nice clump, but is not invasive. The pretty, glossy, foliage stays green until December. It is animal resistant to critters; deer, elk, rabbits and our smaller, furry friends, chipmunks and squirrels. The BEST thing about the Lenten Rose are the fabulous blooms! It begins blooming in late February or early March here in Flagstaff. Each stem holds 3-5 flowers. A large, mature plant can produce up to 30 flower stalks. What a fantastic bouquet they make! The colors are muted shades of yellow, mauve, peach, white with pink, pure white and a spectacular black. Not only are they pretty, and so welcome in early spring, but they LAST! I began bringing them in the house so I could enjoy them. The blooms lasted a full three weeks. You can also cut the individual flowers and float them in a bowl.

Lenten Rose

The down side to this lovely plant is they tend to be pricey and the are very slow growing. It takes 3-5 years to get a good-sized plant.

Liatris

This is a wonderful plant! It grows from a bulb about the size of a nickel and every year the bulbs multiply, much like a daffodil until it forms a large clump. It comes up rather late in the spring sending up slender, low growing foliage. In August, it sends up a tall spike that blooms with dozens of tiny purple feathery flowers that make it look like a purple feather duster. It also comes in white but I don't like the white, it looks like a dirty feather duster.

Russell Lupine and Wild Lupine

Russell lupine is one of my favorites with beautiful spikes in all sorts of color combinations. The leaves are beautiful and a pretty addition to the perennial bed. I have a special area reserved for them. They like protection and only partial sun. They have a very unusual but delight-

Russell Lupine

Ox-Eye Daisies

ful fragrance. The only drawback is they are not long lived. Four to six years is about the most you can hope for.

Wild Blue Lupine is easier to grow and while very pretty, the blooms are not as showy as the Russell Lupine. They do reseed more easily though. They both make a great cut flower.

Ox-eye and Shasta Daisy

Both do very well and are extremely hardy. Ox-eye bloom earlier, in June. They are shorter and while the flowers look identical, the stems are shorter, finer and the flowers smaller. They can re seed prolifically! Shastas bloom in July, are taller with a larger stem and flower. Both are great, and both make good cut flowers.

Penstemon

In Flagstaff, it is hard to beat the Rocky Mountain Penstemon and a host of other Penstemon for a dramatic display. Intense purple stalks bloom in June. Hummingbirds, butterflies and bees love them! The plant is extremely hardy, growing almost anywhere. The leaves are attractive and once the bloom stalk is cut down makes a nice green ground cover. They will do well in the most difficult area of your yard.

Peony

This is another "memory" plant for me. While camping near Telluride, Colorado in the 1980's I struck up a conversation with an elderly woman who was born and raised in Telluride. She ran the museum in town and was a fascinating resource for local history. She had a Victorian garden planted with period flowers around the fence and up the sidewalk of her home. She had several peony plants with flowers the size of saucers with a wonderful fragrance. She graciously cut some for me to take to my campsite. I thought, if they can grow in Telluride at 9,000 feet, they could certainly grow in Flagstaff! Now, I have twenty, white and all shades of pink. They seem to like an east or southern exposure. Give them plenty of water and fertilizer in the spring for the best blooms. This past year I tried dividing them and much to my surprise it was easy and they did beautifully. The old established peony also did well and seemed to appreciate the extra room. They divide much like rhubarb.

Phlox

There are two main types of phlox and I love them both. The creeping phlox, a ground cover is beautiful in the spring as it blooms in lavender, hot pink or white. It is extremely hardy and after blooming remains a nice ground cover. The tall phlox is something I have tried more recently. It grows to about 3 or 4 feet in a variety of colors. The plant is lovely in the garden but I discovered its best virtue several years ago. I wanted to do a bouquet for a baby shower and I wanted it to be spectacular! I picked all my phlox and had it in the kitchen overnight. When I got up the next morning I was overwhelmed with the wonderful fragrance. I began selling the flower in bouquets on my Farmstand and people came back asking for the phlox calling it the "flower that smells so good." They form a nice clump, which comes back bigger each year, and are easy to divide for transplant.

Wood Violet

Violets and all members of the pansy family love our mountain climate, flourishing without much care! They do very well in shade and will re-seed in a rocky area. They come in two colors, purple and white with blue highlights.

Plant Sources

How do you obtain all these great plants without taking out a loan? Start with one garden bed at a time. Then ask a gardener to share! If you have a friend who has a plant you want, ask to trade one of yours or ask for a division. Most gardeners with established gardens are happy to do this, as they need to thin out their own plants anyway. My church, Flagstaff Christian Fellowship sponsors a large garage sale every spring with a selection of perennials for sale. Locals put it on their calendars knowing they can buy plants that are already acclimated to our soil and climate. Plus they are proven winners for Flagstaff. Sometimes when I drive around town I will see a yard and know that it came from the FCF garage sale! My Farmstand has become a great source for perennial flowers. I am always digging them up from my own yard, or ones I have rescued, but more and more people are bringing excess plants from their yards. It is really turning into the "Plant Pound"! If you don't have generous gardening friends, arrange a plant exchange in your neighborhood. Not only will you possibly obtain new plants, but also you might obtain some new friends. For hard to find plants there are great catalogs (listed in the back of the book) to choose from or your local nursery may be able to help. I suggest when purchasing from a nursery, buy the smallest size available and carefully nurture it into a garden trophy. The bigger the plant you purchase the more expensive it will be. Most nurseries put their perennials on sale in the late summer, so this is a good time to buy and a good time to plant.

Keep a sharp watch around your neighborhood. I have often found plants being discarded; just like the day I found the day lilies when I was seven. On one occasion, I found over 200 daffodil bulbs left by the side of the road. Last

DIVIDING BULBS AND PERENNIALS

I have often heard people say, "I don't want anything that has to be divided." Honestly, nothing HAS to be divided, it CAN be divided. You can leave something untouched for decades and it will still bloom. However if you want to give some away or add plants to new beds this is a great way to get new plants. The best time to divide perennials is early spring, as soon as you see them coming up. The bigger the plant, the more difficult to handle and the more stress dividing is on the plant. I usually dig up the whole plant, carefully dividing it into healthy portions. Sometimes roots are so intertwined you have to take a shovel and cut the root ball in half. Soaking the roots in water will also loosen and relax them.

The best time to dig bulbs is in the fall but the problem is, they have died back and I don't know where they are exactly. I have found that digging the bulbs is best done late in the growing season. It stresses them a little but not as stressful as cutting them in half! Dig them up, separate all the bulbs, sometimes as many as 24 in a clump and move them to their new location. Water well! If I am going to sell them I put the whole clump in a pot, water well and wait for them to naturally die back. I tip the pot over, out tumble all the bulbs and they are ready for planting or for sale. I encourage my customers to plant as soon as they buy them, even in June or July. I have heard too many stories of bulbs forgotten in the garage.

year I was walking to the park and a neighbor was digging up her tulips. She had a huge pile of pink tulip bulbs. When I walked back home I stopped and asked her what she was going to do with them. "Throw them out! I don't like pink!" I took them home! I love pink.

Bulbs can be expensive but they all go on sale at the end of the season, usually late November, December, even January. You may find some great deals at this time with bulbs being 50% off, sometimes more. When purchasing very late, the ground may be frozen so I have grown them indoors for the first season. Oh, what glory to have daffodils blooming in February in the house! I plant them in a pot that is at least 10 inches tall. The bulbs sit on top, with only one third in the soil. This leaves almost the entire pot for the extensive root system they will produce. The daffodils started indoors will die back before the ones outdoors and you can easily see where you can add a few more bulbs to your garden. I now have over 2,000 bulbs in the yard and the ditch behind the house with the total cost not being over $200.

There are many ways to cut the price of plants but treat yourself to at least one new plant at FULL PRICE each year!

These plants are some of my favorites and ones that I think most people enjoy and have great success. Additional plants that I think do well are Sweet William, pinks, Veronica, peach leaf bellflower, clematis, butterfly bush, yarrow, California poppies, saliva, Lily of the Valley.

CHAPTER 7: BEST ANNUALS FOR THE MOUNTAINS OF THE SOUTHWEST

If perennials are so great, why bother with annuals? Good question! Perennials by their very nature have a shorter bloom time, usually two weeks, so you have to have a lot of different types to provide a constant bloom. Annuals bloom all summer! Their profuse, spectacular displays with vibrant color add so much to your yard. Many gardeners use the cut flowers in bouquets or munch on those that are edible.

When planting your garden beds, remember that blue and purple shades tend to disappear in the landscape. Keep them close to the front door, paths or sidewalk so you can enjoy them. Hot shades like yellow, pink and reds jump out from almost anywhere.

Cosmos

Cosmos

Cosmos are fun to grow from seed creating a tall display of graceful, green foliage with bright blossoms in shades of pink and white. They are hardy in areas where other flowers struggle, and look especially nice mixed in with veggies or with spring bulbs. They easily re-seed and return year after year. They are super easy to transplant. The new variety of Picotee cosmos are delightful with pink edging on the white flowers, stripping and variegated shades in one blossom.

Marigolds

Marigolds are easy to grow and they come in all sizes with different configurations on their petals. They help deter some garden pests and they are easy for kids to grow. I don't like them. I don't like how they look and I don't like how they smell. The same lady who was pulling out her entire bed of pink tulips has a yard full of them. She likes yellow and orange. I have to admit her yard is pretty and festive. Check the garden catalog for a greater variety than is found in the nursery.

Nasturtiums

This is another tasty flower, although spicier than the pansy family. They are easy to plant with large seeds and easy to grow in poor soil. The circular leaves add visual interest and the flowers make nice fresh bouquets. Some varieties are small and bushy, some have variegated leaves, and my favorite is a 'trailing nasturtium', which can grow 20 feet in a summer. I use it to climb fences and trellises. I have not had good luck growing them in pots, and I don't know why. They prefer part shade to full sun.

The Pansy Family

Pansies, including Violas and Johnny Jump-ups are cold hardy, and fun to look at with those cute little faces. The edible blossoms are perfect and delicious for salads, vegetable or fruit trays and desserts. Gardeners grow them for their culinary uses if nothing else. Different colors have different tastes. They are often the first to emerge in the spring often peeping through the snow showers. Technically they are annuals, but because they freely re-seed you may have them popping up all over the yard for years to come.

Petunias

Nothing is as spectacular as a pot or basket of petunias! Several years ago, I was visiting my daughter in Indiana. We drove the entire length of the state through small towns looking at farms and a few cemeteries, making it a perfect day for me! The highlight was when we stopped at an Amish nursery. The owner's home was right next door and hanging from the second story balcony was a plant that LOOKED like a petunia, but it was hanging down about four feet and literally covered with about 500 blooms. I asked, "what is that?" The woman replied, "It's a petunia. I planted it from seed in February. The secret is to water it every day and give it Miracle-Gro every two weeks." There you have it, the secret for growing petunias! I tried her advice that summer and sure enough they were the best petunias I had ever grown. They also make a great border for taller perennials,

Petunias

adding a bright splash of color.

Snapdragons

Another cold hardy plant, snapdragons, are easy to care for and produce loads of blooms all summer and well into fall. They are great in bouquets or by themselves. They tolerate shade well and will even last two years or more if they are planted in a protected place. I had two pots full of snapdragons last summer that I have been overwintering in a back room. They are doing great and I think I will get another productive season from them.

Sunflowers

Sunflowers

One snowy winter day in January, I was thumbing through one of my favorite seed catalogs, from Harris Seeds, and decided to call the nursery with a question about a variety of squash. The woman who answered the phone didn't know the answer and asked, "Would you like to speak to our resident farmer?" "Sure," I said. What she couldn't see was how I rolled my eyes and shook my head while thinking; they don't have a resident farmer. When Jeff Werner answered the phone and asked, "So, I understand you're a farmer." "I am," he replied. "I had a 500-acre organic farm. Its smaller now, but still keeps me busy. I sell my produce at a Farmers Market."

I could not believe my good fortune. A grower who sells his product AND knows both ends of the business. I hit him with a barrage of questions and gained so much valuable information. He was an incredible resource. Two hours later he was able to escape my phone call. He told me he could only talk that long in the slow months. During the conversation, I asked what flowers he sold at the Farmers Market. He said sunflowers are the number one seller and his favorite was a bi-color from Harris Seeds called Pro-Cut bi-color. "I don't get it with sunflowers," I said. "I see customers buying them at local Farmers Market but why do people buy them?" "They make people happy," he answered. Okay, that was a good reason. I ordered a package of 250 seeds. For some reason, I went wild and planted the whole package. I had never grown a sunflower and wasn't sure what they would need or what they would do. I planted them all over the front and back yard, the side yard, in pots, close together, far apart, good soil, poor soil, even transplanted them to see how they would fare. They were great fun! The seedlings came up well, grew quickly, and started to bloom. All the blossoms faced the street, like they were showing off. People stopped their cars to look at sunflowers. People brought their cameras and were taking pictures, asking for seeds for the next year. The cut flowers sold like crazy. "Sunflowers," I thought, "DO make people happy. They are making ME happy!" This variety bloomed relatively early in August. The incredibly strong stems stood tall and did not need to be staked for support. The plants produced one giant flower and a few additional smaller blooms on the same stem. I found even the plants in poor soil, partial shade or too close together, produced a nice sized flower that sometimes were more manageable than the giants produced in the ideal conditions. I find they last a long time, up to two weeks in the yard or as a cut flower. They are an excellent flower for children to try.

Sweet Peas

I grew sweet peas, an old favorite, for my wedding bouquet. Just like the delicious snap peas, sweet peas can be started very early as they are frost proof and need a wire fence to climb. Some of the newer varieties have had that wonderful aroma bred out of them, so if you want fragrance, look for the old varieties. Soak the seeds for 48 hours and plant fairly close together. St. Patrick's Day, March 17 is the traditional day for planting Sweet Peas. Many seeds will last for years but this is one case (T&E) where you cannot save seeds for more than one year. Be extravagant and plant ALL your seeds at once, as most will not be viable the next year.

Zinnias

Zinnias are a great flower! There are several varieties from the smallest, Lilliput, with half inch blossoms, to the giants sporting a nice cutting flower that can be up to five inches across. There are also cactus types, striped and speckled. I have always grown them, planting the seed directly into the ground. I think they would do better if started inside and then put out. They need a bit longer growing season with rich soil and as much warmth as you can provide.

The annuals mentioned above are some of my favorites. Others I have grown are Dahlias, Bells of Ireland, Bachelor Buttons, Larkspur, Shirley Poppies, California Poppies, Calendula, and Clarkia.

CHAPTER 8: BEST VEGETABLES FOR FLAGSTAFF AND THE MOUNTAIN SOUTHWEST

There is nothing more satisfying in the world (except raising children!) than growing a vegetable from seed and eating the fruit of your labor. I still remember jumping up out of bed as a five year old to run outside to see if the squash were coming up. Even after 60 years, it is still a thrill to see the little squash seedlings poking through the dark earth. Many of the problems that people experience in growing vegetables are self-imposed.

Remember 3 simple things:

1.   No region in the world has "perfect conditions" for growing everything. Everyone faces an obstacle in growing annuals and vegetables. Pests vary from one place to another. Conditions are too wet or too dry, too hot or too cold. The soil may be poor. We all have our challenges! Don't lament where you live, embrace it!

2.   Concentrate on the vegetables suited to your area. Ninety percent of them should be things that thrive where you live. It is okay to have some fun and excitement and try new things, but failure isn't fun. You can't grow everything!

3.   Learn from mistakes. Every year is another opportunity to learn something new. No experience is ever lost, so with an attitude to learn, you can reap great benefits year after year. When something doesn't do well, ask yourself, why? Do I need to improve the soil? Try a different exposure? Change how I water? Try a different variety? Ask questions to more experienced gardeners in your area to gain knowledge: gardeners LOVE to talk about their gardens.

How do you determine what to grow?

Start by observing what grows well in your neighborhood. As you walk around your neighborhood, look for particular plants, an indicator these plants will do well in your area. Veggies are more difficult to observe because they are often in the backyard, out of sight. Again, gardeners LOVE to talk about their gardens, what they grow and what does well for them. Begin by engaging experienced gardeners in conversations. Generally, they will be more than happy to share their experiences with you. Local nurseries can be helpful, as well as the master gardeners in your area. Western States have a cooperative extension office with expert advice. The Internet has become a great resource for the home gardener. Nothing, however, beats personal experience for learning and understanding the preference of a particular vegetable. I will start the discussion with cold weather veggies and move to the warmer ones.

Asparagus

Asparagus emerging in the spring.

Forty years ago, it was my dream to have an asparagus farm. Everyone I told, laughed at this, but I was dead serious. I worked hard to build the beds and made bed after bed, filling them with asparagus plants. I got the plants from various places. My dad had brought home seeds from a Flagstaff pioneer in the 1960's and planted them. We had a beautiful bed in our backyard. I got most of my plants from volunteers from that bed. I ordered some from catalogs plus had a few "rescue plants" I found around town or were given to me. I spent a couple of years building the beds by adding lots of manure and compost before the plants went in. I managed to get up to 400 plants! Then disaster struck. Five years of drought, grasshoppers, then an aphid infestation took its toll. In the end, I lost over three quarters of my plants with only seventy-five surviving.

I was so discouraged, but I consoled myself with the thought that at least I still had the good soil and it would be usable for other plants. I filled the beds with perennials and veggies and gave up on my dream.

For five more years, the seventy five plants limped along not getting much love or attention. One summer, I had extra time and began to rehabilitate them. I gave them each a rock; this provides added warmth and helps to conserve water. I top dressed them with cow pies I picked up in the woods. I weeded them and gave them all a good soaking. Finally, I treated them to a dose of Miracle-Gro after the harvest was over.

I spotted a few volunteers and moved them to an "asparagus nursery" where they could receive more attention and better care. I began to notice these seedlings were far superior to any asparagus I had ever grown. I began to think I had accidentally developed a new strain more suited to Flagstaff. I started saving seeds in earnest, and planted away. I hope to have 200 plants by next year. In two years, I hope to be selling seeds and one year-old plants calling them "Julie's Flagstaff

Select".

THE DREAM IS BACK!

Growing Asparagus

Asparagus is a perennial vegetable high in nutrients and very long lived, with some living to be over 100 years old! It is considered an heirloom plant because of its longevity and the same plant will provide food for many generations. Because it will remain in one place for many decades, it is of great importance that the plants are placed in the best possible soil you can give them. A deep bed loaded with compost and manure is what they really like. It is also important to keep the bed free of weeds. Weeding is easiest in the spring before the spears appear which happens in my area around April 1. I have found they do well along a fence line, and can grow up to six feet tall. The harvest takes place in spring. It is best to wait until the plants are three years old to begin to harvest.

The first couple of years, other things can be planted in between the baby plants, beans, flowers, all kinds of things. I plant them closer than is usually suggested as garden space is at a premium. I plant them about one foot apart. I also don't plant quite as deep as is usually suggested, as they would reach down to bad Flagstaff clay. I do make sure they are in a depression, and fill it with manure gradually as the plant grows. I like to transplant a two-year-old plant into the permanent bed. I do it in late March or early April. As soon as the plants are dug up from my asparagus nursery, I soak them in a tray of water. I spread the roots out in all directions in the hole and cover them with about 4 inches of dirt and give them a good watering and Miracle-Gro. Even if you are organic, you can use Miracle-Gro that first year as you will not be eating it. I think it does help to give them Miracle-Gro once each year after the harvest as a special treat. If you are committed to organic, then give them a good dose of manure tea.

Once the spears on any plant are smaller than a pencil, I let them go. All plants should be allowed to grow by the middle of June. Harvesting too long will stress or even kill a plant. The plants then will form a large feathery fern like plant that is pretty to look at. Cosmos interspersed in the plants will grow up with them, making it look like the asparagus is blooming! Along the chain link fence, I plant peas every year with the asparagus. The peas provide additional nitrogen for the asparagus and everyone seems happy! The plants should be watered and tended throughout the season. In the fall, the plants turn a gorgeous yellow and the female plants will have bright red berries. The berries are thick and sticky and birds will enjoy them. In each one, there are 3-5 jet black shiny seeds. It is vital that the fronds not be cut down till very late fall, as the foliage is feeding the roots for next year's harvest. I usually leave them alone and do the clean-up in the spring. Asparagus prefers full sun, but I have very little of that and other plants need it more. It seems to do well in part shade.

Beans

At one time, the predominate vegetable crop grown in Flagstaff was beans- not green beans, but pinto beans. The neighborhoods known as Upper and Lower Greenlaw, Doney Park and much of Sunnyside were bean fields. Beans do well in Flagstaff! Bush beans have a short growing season. The plants are extremely sensitive to frost and very hard to cover. As they need warm soil to germinate, I have learned to plant them in mid-June (T&E). They can tolerate part-shade and be tucked here and there in the garden. They can be planted where daffodils or other bulbs are just dying back. They can be grouped or planted in rows. They add nitrogen to the soil so they are very beneficial, like peas. My favorite place to plant them is in the "hose guard pots" (see Composting chapter) placed strategically to keep my hose in line. Planted in pots, the beans are much easier to pick, they don't get dirty, or have slugs or other insects eating them (I hate that!).

Pole beans are fun to grow, they taste great and are easy to pick. As their name implies they need a pole. They do not like a chain fence; the diamond shaped links confuse them. You can use a trellis or string tied to a fence. I have used stakes, poles, and wedding arbors that were snagged out of the trash or at a garage sale. The vines usually don't need help attaching to the trellis but if they do, they curl around the support counter clockwise. In order to get the best harvest they do need to be planted earlier than bush beans. Since they are usually in a more confined area, they are a little easier to cover.

Do not soak beans before planting.

Cabbage

My grandmother loved growing cabbage in her half-block farm in downtown Flagstaff. It was her signature vegetable. She became well known for her "baby cabbages". In the early 1900's, families were often large and cabbage became a stable in their diet. Cabbage could be stored easily without refrigeration in root cellars through the winter. My grandmother was familiar with the requirements for growing cabbage due to early years as a peasant farmer in Sweden. Cabbage became a popular American vegetable unlike her beloved rutabagas, which she grew and fed to her six children. There wasn't much of a market for rutabagas. My grandmother started cabbage in a cold frame then moved it to the garden when warmer weather arrived. I find it very beautiful and it is highly nutritious. Cabbage needs good soil and full sun.

Kale

I first tried kale due to a farmstand customer request. My first thoughts after trying it were, "Good grief, who is eating this other than the insects?" I have found that by nibbling from time to time I have acquired a taste for it. Olive Garden restaurants serve a popular soup, using kale as one of the main ingredients. I grew mostly the Red Russian. Ten years ago I could barely give it away, now there is a huge demand. Kale has become very desirable because people have learned of its super food qualities and also juicing has opened up a new door for kale.

I was having lots of problems growing it. This past March, while riding the train to Indiana, I became friends with an Amish man from Michigan. I told him of my difficulties and asked for his suggestions. He told me to try the Siberian variety and to try starting them indoors. He said they didn't do well directly planted and that they are quite sensitive when young. His cousin's Amish seed store was only an hour from my daughter's house. That was an adventure! He graciously invited me to visit anytime I was in the area. I was able to visit Andrew and Lena and their 12 children on their farm in Michigan five months later! I had an enjoyable day, the most delicious meal, and an unforgettable farm tour.

Kale needs a good amount of sun, the best, composted soil you can give it, plenty of water and lots of space. They need to be a minimum of 12 inches apart- they will grow into their space! As I mentioned earlier, the bugs go for kale in a big way. They will arrive in droves to munch on your kale bed. Putting the plants out later when they are a little bigger helps greatly, but you still have to watch them all season! Black Corn Fleas seem to have radar fixed onto kale and can quickly decimate a plant. Grasshoppers will devour them as well. Aphids will congregate there. I'm surprised at how insects prefer kale to any other vegetable in my garden. They must know kale is one of the most nutritious vegetables on the planet. Kale kept many people alive during the hardships of World War II.

Lettuce

Lettuce is another very hardy vegetable that does extremely well in cool weather. It looks so delicate and fragile, but it is not! It can be planted in early April and will take very cold weather and need little protection, except maybe from damaging rain or hail. I prefer to plant seeds directly into the soil. Lettuce seeds sometimes pool into one area, but they can be transplanted easily. Most seed companies have a lettuce mix or you can make your own using your favorite varieties. I DID NOT LIKE the mesclun mix as some of the greens are bitter and have too strong of a taste. The lettuce mix will contain only lettuce and is delicious. With a mix, you can try a nice variety of different lettuce, all beautiful to look at in the salad bowl. Don't forget to add some edible flowers. If you want lettuce all season, you will have to plant a second crop later in the season as the first crop will not make it through the summer. It will begin to bolt, usually in late July (T&E). July 1st is an ideal time to put in a second planting. To harvest, never pull up from the roots. Instead, give it a haircut, leaving at least a couple of inches on the plant to sprout new leaves. You can do this several times through the season. Another option is to carefully go through and pick just the outer, biggest leaves, efficient but more time consuming. Lettuce does great in all types of containers, I recommend the lettuce mix from Pinetree Seeds, the most popular thing they sell. The one-ounce package is the best value.

Colorful Glaskins Perpetual Rhubarb. This plant is one-years old.

Rhubarb: The perfect plant for Flagstaff!

For years, one lone rhubarb plant existed in a garden bed off my back porch, unloved, unnoticed and unappreciated. When a neighbor discovered I had it, she came over in June and harvested it for strawberry-rhubarb pie and to use with a variety of fruits to make jam. When I opened my farmstand, rhubarb was hit or miss, so I decided to make a sign that said, "RHUBARB AVAILABLE UPON REQUEST." By this time I had divided the first plant which was green

(Victoria) into four plants, and bought a red plant (Chipman's Canadian Red).

About three years ago, a couple from Phoenix was at a vacation rental in the Cheshire neighborhood and they were ecstatic that I had rhubarb. As I was out back harvesting, another couple came to the farmstand and asked, "Where's Julie?"

"Oh, she's in her backyard getting us some rhubarb."

"Rhubarb? What are you going to do with it?"

"Make rhubarb sauce. We cut it up and cook it down like applesauce, add some sugar or honey and use it as a topping for vanilla ice cream. It's so yummy!"

I returned with the rhubarb, and the second couple said, "We would like some rhubarb, too."

This was repeated over and over again during the summer and thus began what I can only describe as a rhubarb craze at my farmstand. I thought, "I need to get about 100 rhubarb plants!" Now the problem is that rhubarb plants are pricey. I got my original plants from a seed catalog at $12/each. I had been told that you couldn't get rhubarb seeds, and I had never seen any. Then I saw seeds in a Pinetree Garden seed catalog. Ah ha, I knew there had to be seeds! Last year, I ordered a packet of seed of Glaskins Perpetual, a British heirloom and by the end of the summer, I had 12 big, beautiful rhubarb plants, some two feet in diameter, for $1.75! All twelve came back this year and 30 more are waiting on the porch for permanent homes in the yard once the weather warms up a bit.

Advantages of Rhubarb

- Technically a vegetable, it is loaded with vitamin K & C, and antioxidants.
- Rhubarb loves the cold! It does not tolerate heat, so Flagstaff is perfect.
- It is a long-lived perennials, living for decades.
- It's pretty! It emerges from the ground like a nest of pink balls, about the same time as daffodils. The plant grows rapidly and is ready to harvest May or June. The plant looks good all summer and is sometimes mistaken for squash.
- It can be harvested all at once in May or June, and a second lighter cutting can be taken in July. Or stalks can be harvested

a few at a time through the summer. Leaves are poisonous.

- It does best in good soil and lots of water but will still grow well in average soil and minimum care.
- It will grow in full sun or part-shade.

Besides the sauce, jam, and pie mentioned above, there is also rhubarb cake, rhubarb sorbet and rhubarb tea! It can be used as a topping for meat, in soups, and stews. The sauce can be eaten alone, as one of my customers testified, "I made sauce and set it on the table for my three young children. I thought what they didn't eat my husband and I could finish off. When I turned around, it was gone!"

Rhubarb Sauce

1 pound rhubarb, chopped in about 1/2" pieces

1 ¼ cup sugar

1 TBSP cornstarch

(This is a rough estimate, just add some sugar *or honey* until you like the way it tastes)

Place rhubarb in a medium saucepan with a small amount of water, about ½ inch. Add sugar and boil. Simmer for about 12 minutes or until rhubarb is tender. At this point, it is all about preference. I like it with nice big chunks, so I leave it as is. But you could put it in a food processor and blend it until smooth.

Snap Peas

Delicious snap peas should be in every garden! Making use of our cool weather with these little treasures, I plant mine along both chain link and solid wood fences (the wood fence has a wire trellis, a 3-inch wire fencing scrap pulled from the trash). This is one of the coldest areas in the yard and the peas love it. Provided there is not two feet of snow on the ground, I plant in mid-March, sowing the peas very thickly, only one to two inches apart, in a six-inch wide trench. I soak the peas for 48 hours before planting. This helps to offset the difficulties in keeping the soil moist. They are not fazed by freezing nights and continue to grow. I have NEVER covered or protected the peas in any way, no matter the conditions. Usually they will climb by themselves, but sometimes I give them a little help. I either help them curl around the wire, or if they are really stubborn, I use a twist tie to secure them.

In mid-summer, they take a "break" when it gets too warm. Keep watering, as they will resume blooming when the rains start and produce peas till frost. They sometimes have topped a six-foot fence. They will do well in part shade. There are a number of varieties but I use Sugar Snap from Harris Seeds, buying a 5-pound seed packet, which lasts me a decade.

Spinach

Spinach thrives in cold weather and is super easy to grow. It will also return for a short while the second year. This can be planted directly into the garden bed. The seeds are easy to handle and do not need to be soaked.

Summer Squash

My favorite vegetable is summer squash, as I just love watching it grow! The seeds can be put out directly once the danger of frost is passed. I need it sooner for my farmstand, so I start them indoors. I soak the seeds for 24 hours then place them in a shallow tray filled with potting soil, barely covering them. They go behind the wood-burning stove where they germinate in 4-7 days. As soon as I see a seed is viable, out it goes to the garden bed. I put a seed on each side of the already prepared bed with a water jug in place, give it a good watering and cover it with a plastic bin. I scoop dirt around the edges of the bin so cold air doesn't get in and place a medium sized rock on top. The rock needs to be heavy enough to hold the bin down in the wind storm that will inevitably come, but not so heavy that it would break through the plastic. Once in place, it can be left alone for up to two weeks. Lift up the bin to give a good watering occasionally and they are on their own in there. Watering needs to increase as the weather warms. I do this usual-ly the first part of April and I am harvesting squash in mid-June! The leaves will get very large and begin touch-ing the tops of the bins. The day before you remove the bin, give the plant a deep drenching; soak it well to thoroughly hydrate

What's in the jug? Hundreds of people stop to ask if it's Miracle-Gro or anti-freeze, but it's black food coloring!

the plant (T&E). Try to do all this when the wind is a minimum. Remember, these guys have been living a "greenhouse life". They are not used to wind or direct sun. The following morning, early, remove the bin. Watch the plant through the day for any signs of stress, wilting or leaves drying out. If you see this, the bin can go back on or cover with a cardboard box or lawn chair to protect them. It only takes one or two days at the most for the squash plant to acclimate and they are off to the races!

Another thing that will help heat-loving plants is black plastic mulch or fabric to hold water and warm their roots. A number of years ago, I visited a garden in Taylor, Arizona. This elderly man had converted his entire front yard to vegetables with a small flower garden on the side. It was beautiful! I told him I had come all the way from Flagstaff to see his garden. It made his day! His wife, wondering why he had not come inside for lunch, came out looking for him. He told her, "She came all the way from Flagstaff to see my garden!" His wife looked at him in total unbelief and said, "She did not!" I assured her that indeed, it was true. This man was a wealth of information. He showed me the benefit of black plastic, saying that he used it every year on his squash giving him a huge advantage.

Summer squash is a very needy vegetable! They require full sun with lots of organic material especially manure. They need to be watered on a consistent schedule. They are extremely frost sensitive. To ensure continued production, keep picking the squash. And in some areas, watch out for the nasty "squash beetles" that multiply quickly by laying their eggs under the leaves. You'll know if you have them when you see a piece of squash that has suddenly withered. The best method for eradicating them is to squish them and their eggs by hand.

Zucchini Elite staying warm with a jug.

My absolute favorite variety is "Zucchini Elite" from Harris Seeds. This is a perfect squash plant as it produces loads of nice, straight zucchini. The plant has a habit of growing straight up, resembling a "zucchini tree". This is advantageous for me as it allows me to move quickly between the plants for harvesting. Another good producer is "Golden Rod," also from Harris Seeds. This one is the deepest yellow I have ever seen and is a good producer.

You will notice in the seed catalogs the description, "novelty squashes". Remember, as with the perennial plants, altering the genetics weakens the overall plant. You won't get the same yield and hardiness as you would in the tried and true varieties.

Swiss Chard

Swiss Chard is delightful to grow and a great vegetable for cold weather! I use several varieties. The white chard grows the fastest and produces the most. The 'Northern Lights' with red, pink, orange, and yellow stalks is just so pretty, it has to be included. Again, it is important to soak the seeds before planting. Chard will also tolerate some shade but not as much as the lettuce.

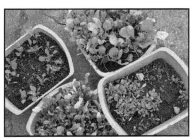

Baby swiss chard almost ready for transplanting to the garden. Growing in rescued hospital bins.

I have found that starting these inside helps as well. I plant them thickly in a tray at least six inches deep. They stay outside on the porch most of the time but I bring them in with severe cold or bad weather. Chard will often come up the second year and before it bolts and goes to seed, you can get a decent crop. By the time the chard is about ready to bolt, my little plants in the tray are big enough to go outside into the garden. It is not long before I am harvesting them, making a near continuous supply of chard for my farmstand customers. Harvest only the outer, largest leaves, taking care not to cut the interior stalk. I like to harvest at about 8-10 inches, as it is most tender at this point. Chard needs a very nutritious composted soil and thorough watering. I plant them about 6-8 inches apart. Lime added to the soil will increase leaf production.

Tomatoes

The best place for tomatoes in Flagstaff is next to the house on the east or south side of your home. They like to be in a five-gallon or larger BLACK pot to warm their roots. In some of the warmer areas of town, friends have success growing tomatoes directly in their gardens.

- Four things tomatoes love: good compost, heat, water, and protection
- Four things tomatoes hate: wind, cold, sporadic watering, hard rain or hail

Planting Tomatoes

In May, take your well-watered plant (grown from seed or purchased) and clip leaves among the stem, not too close, leaving the top leaves intact. Gently turn the pot over and let the plant slide out. Bury as far down in either the five gallon pot or the ground as possible, leaving the top leaves above the soil line. If planted in pots, the pot should be deeper than it is wide. Gently fill the holes with the best soil available. I prefer a combination of compost, manure, and good soil. Water several times in the process. The stem will quickly root where you have clipped the branches, creating a two-tier set of roots.

> To the first person who said "Pull up your tomatoes and hang them in the garage", I would like to hunt them down and make them clean up the mess in thousands of garages across America. I would force them to eat pithy tomatoes with skins as tough as leather. Instead, pick ALL of your tomatoes, and place them in a box, brown paper bag or cupboard. They WILL ripen quickly and be delicious! For the smallest green tomatoes, check out the recipes online for fried green tomatoes. Again, delicious!

After filling the hole, place a sturdy (large size) tomato cage around the plant (tomatoes in pots also appreciate a gallon jug of water), sinking the tines into the soil. For extra support, a wood or metal stake can go along the edge of the pot. Water daily. Using a clothespin or clip, secure a sheet over the back of the plants next to the house. One sheet will cover 4-5 plants. Uncover the plants in the morning, cover again at night as long as there is a threat of frost. I prefer to continue doing this until mid-June to give the plants extra warmth. I sometimes leave them covered for several days at a time during a cold snap or with high winds. Unfortunately, it is not uncommon in Flagstaff during May or June.

For a VERY hard freeze, use crumpled newspaper or cotton rags around the stem. Add a cloth over the interior lower rung of the cage, with an additional sheet or light blanket on top. You can also use a string of Christmas lights along the cages for added warmth. I don't use "wall of water" but many people swear by them. Try them and see how you like them. They actually can remain on the plant for an entire season.

I sing a little goodnight song to them in the evening while covering and a good morning song to being their day. Singing to your tomatoes is optional!

In no time, you will have a robust tomato plant.

Tomato Plants by Seed

There are wonderful varieties to choose from that the nurseries don't carry. Catalogs classify tomatoes as either "determinate" or "indeterminate":

> Determinate = compact
>
> Indeterminate = large, climbing, and spreading

Considering our short growing season, select a variety with a maturation or growing season no longer than 70 days. It is fun and very rewarding to grow your tomatoes from seeds. If started early, you can have a good sized, hearty plant in May. I plant the seeds as early as January 1st. Consider planting at least by Valentine's Day if you want mature plants for your mountain garden by May.

How to plant the seeds:

Using a quart-sized pot or slightly smaller size, fill with good compost mixed with a little perlite or potting soil to lighten the planting compound. Place pot(s) in a plastic tray, storage box, or hospital wash basin, etc. Water thoroughly, leaving the mix damp. Follow directions on the seed packet. I use a pencil to make an indentation. I plant two seeds per pot about a quarter inch apart. Sometimes only one comes up, but if both are hearty, I let them both grow. If you are trying several varieties, mark them with plant markers. As heat rises, place the tray in the warmest spot in the house: behind the wood burning stove or near the dryer on a shelf. Remember to keep them moist. The seedling takes about a week to emerge. As soon as the first one is up, move it or the whole tray to your warmest, sunniest window. They will remain there until they are planted. They may need a bit of liquid fertilizer while in the window. If they become long and leggy, pinch back each branch to help produce a thick, sturdy stem.

Buying Plants

I recommend nursery plants for the novice gardeners for the first two years. The bigger the plant, the more expensive it will be. Avoid the varieties that require a longer maturation like "Beef Steak" and

"Big Boy". With our short growing season, you'll have better results with tomatoes that require about 60 days to maturation. Some of my favorites include "Early Girl", "Celebrity", or "Bush Goliath". "Sweet 100" or "Sweet Million" for cherry tomatoes. Ultimately, my favorite is, "Celebrity".

After planting, remove the blossoms on the smaller tomato plants so the plant will concentrate the nutrients it receives toward growing.

Tips

For increased production, brush tomato blossoms with a paint-brush or Q-tip. If you are growing tomatoes in pots, recognize that even with the best intentions, pots dry out. You will notice the soil pulling away from the edge of the pot. Don't quickly dump a gallon of water in the pot, as the water will run straight through. Pour a gallon, one cup at a time, s l o w l y onto the tomatoes to allow it to rehydrate. It may require two to three gallons.

If the frost catches your tender plants before all the tomatoes have ripened, pick the green fruit and either lay it out on the newspaper or store in a paper bag. The tomatoes will continue to ripen off the vine. Check the tomatoes every day, using them as they ripen.

Winter Squash and Pumpkins

Next to the Summer Squash, these are my favorite. I love watching those vines grow. Growing conditions are almost the same as with summer squash, but they are much hardier than their summer cousins. They can tolerate more shade, less water and poorer soil. Gardeners have an advantage in leaving the winter squash for harvesting till the end of the season after frost has taken out most of the rest of my garden. They keep for months, hence the name "winter", allowing you to eat them during the cold months when all else is gone. The vines of the winter squash love to roam all over the place, climbing fences, growing across the driveways, your lawn or the neighbor's lawn. Give them room to grow.

Decorative gourds are fun to grow! They are in the same family as the squashes. I have noticed a distinct difference between the sexes in their reaction to the gourds. EVERY woman says, "Oh, look at those cute little gourds, they are so pretty!" EVERY man looks intently at them, studies them, and says, "Can you eat them?" When I say no, I can watch their curiosity getting the best of them. Then they ask,

"Why do you grow them?" Since they are not edible, I use fertilizer in growing them to enormous lengths, just for fun.

The Good News and Bad News about Root Crops

Let's define "root crops". These are any crop with the primary vegetable growing underground. This includes beets, turnips, garlic, onions, parsnips, rutabagas, carrots, and potatoes.

First, the GOOD news. Root crops are very cold hardy. They can be planted early and harvested late. We need not worry about covering or protecting them from frost. That is good news for mountain gardeners! They are relatively pest-free and easy to grow. They also will tolerate part shade, another positive. With beets and turnips, we get a bonus; as the green leafy tops of these plants are delicious.

Now the BAD news. The very fact they are growing four to ten inches deep underground is a serious problem when you are dealing with poor soil. As I mentioned in the section on soil, in Flagstaff, we have "various forms of rock" rather than soil. Compost will certainly solve the problem, but that requires a lot of compost or manure! Best to save the compost for the high maintenance plants. I have found sand is helpful in loosening the soil and is very inexpensive. Pick up a load from your local building material suppliers or order a good amount from the local "dirt guy". After he dumps a pile at the end of your driveway, you can use some for a sandbox. Maybe a neighbor or two would go in on it with you, as they plan their projects.

Novelty Crops

I call these novelty crops because it will be a novelty if you get anything at harvest time! These crops are not made for this area. They were made for somewhere else- Yuma, Camp Verde, and Southern California. Probably for that very reason, people are simply compelled to try to grow them and love the challenge.

Broccoli and Cauliflower

Surprised I am including these? They should do well in a mountain climate, as they are cold and hardy. They take up a fair amount of space and produce what seems to me a very small amount of produce for the space and effort required. They might be fun to try as an experiment, but if you do plant them carefully consider your use of garden space.

Garden pests do seem to love broccoli and cauliflower. Finding a green worm in your veggies is a bit unappetizing. Even with our minimal insect problem in Flagstaff, if there is an insect, it will devour these, so check out some of the organic pest controls. Sometimes it is easier to just pick the pest off the produce and squish it. Some sources recommend that you do not plant broccoli and cauliflower in the same space as previously held by the cabbage family. The seeds are fairly easy to manage and can be sown directly into warm soil, spacing plants 18-24 inches apart. The stalk emerges from the warm soil and the leaves begin to spread outward with the head in the center. The spreading leaves may touch but should not be too crowded. After cutting the central head, side shoots will emerge, extending the harvest if the gardener is diligent in cutting them, rather than allowing the plant to go to seed.

Corn

Corn will grow here and is great fun, especially for children. I think people feel a garden isn't really a garden without corn! The biggest problem with corn is that it takes up a lot of space on small lots. Remember, you should not plant corn in a straight row, as it needs to cross-pollinate. Corn needs to be planted in a block. As the tassel matures, the pollen drifts down to the corn silk, which has emerged, from the ear of the corn. Each silk pollinated, will result in a full kernel on the ear of the corn! That is why you sometimes see homegrown corn that is very blotchy with missing kernels, due to poor pollination. To assist the pollination, lightly grasp and strip the pollen from the top of the stalk. Sprinkle the pollen onto the silk emerging from each ear.

Corn also needs a fair amount of water and draws lots of nutrients out of the soil. You can make better use of your space by planting pole beans with the corn, which will climb the stalks. Pumpkins planted nearby will wind their way through the stalks. Master Gardener, Jim Mast, grew corn successfully here for years and recommends Mother's Day weekend as the time to plant your corn. There are all sorts of new varieties and many suited for northern gardens.

Cucumbers

My own miserable experience with cucumbers has put them in this category. I have tried multiple varieties. I have tried every warm spot in my yard. Most years, the plants don't even live long enough to have a flower much less a cucumber. Once, when I was lamenting the dilemma to a farmstand customer and blaming it on living in Cheshire, the woman who lives directly behind me said, "Last year we had so many I didn't know what to do with them!" I was surprised she was still standing after the withering glance I threw her way! I know people in Flagstaff's "banana belt" who grow them and others scattered around town, but there are many like myself, who have not had any luck with them.

Try starting them indoors two weeks early. Plant the seedlings in a sunny area and place a hot cap over the plant for the first couple of weeks. My fellow gardener, David, insists on starting his cucumbers directly in the warm soil. That choice may depend on your particular micro-climate. Give them lots of water once they start to set fruit. As with squash, black plastic and water jugs may be helpful.

Peppers

Hatch, New Mexico, chili capital of the world! A visit to Hatch will help you understand why we have an uphill battle growing peppers. In Hatch, summer temperatures are in the 90's with lows dropping to the 60's. There is abundant water from the Rio Grande and the soil is loose sand.

Everything they have, we don't! You can provide water and amend the soil with organic material, even add sand, but HEAT is not easy to manufacture. My friend, David, has successfully grown all types of peppers in Flagstaff and says that the secret is in keeping the plastic "wall of water" around them for the entire summer. It is important to open the wall to full width once they begin to emerge from it to ensure good air circulation and allow the peppers to be pollinated. Black plastic also helps and the two can be used together. David has some pepper plants up against a rock wall to keep them warmer at night. Like tomatoes, they may benefit from growing in a black pot. Obviously, they need to go in the ground as plants, either plants you buy or start inside yourself. Increase pollination with the use of a small paintbrush on the blossoms, which open mid-morning.

There are so many varieties of peppers I have lost track of them! From small to large, hot to mild, in every color imaginable. What you grow will depend on what your intended use and what you like to eat. David's favorite varieties are "Goliath hybrid", "Volcano", "Banana Pepper", "Fat 'n Sassy", "Costa Rican Sweet" (red), and "Golden Giant Hybrid" sweet pepper. David gets most of his peppers and tomato seeds from "Totally Tomatoes".

Watermelon and Cantaloupe

Melons require heat, warm nights and lots of water. There are some varieties in the catalogs that have been hybridized for colder climates. With a lot of care and extra attention, it can be done but not well.

Some Quick Tips on Herbs

Parsley: does extremely well here and is cold hardy. Try it indoors in a pot throughout the winter.

Basil: you can't give it too much heat! Do whatever you need to keep it warm, at least 50 degrees at night. Basil won't resent getting up to 100 degrees during the day. Stick with the common Genoa Basil for the best results.

Dill: easy at 7,000 feet, easily re-seeds.

Rosemary: If you bring this tender perennial in each fall, it could live for years.

Cilantro: you need to plant successively to ensure a steady supply during the growing season. Once cilantro bolts seemingly overnight, pull it up.

Lavender: does well here.

Catmint: known as "catnip" when dried, is a lovely flowering shrub and provides entertainment for your cat. I have a friend whose cat sits right in the middle of the mint, eyes closed in sheer ecstasy.

CHAPTER 9: PESTS

Pests

Here are some simple, cost effective and hilarious methods to rid you of pests that come to the garden. Because I garden organically and I am cheap, most of the commercial products on the market are not mentioned here. Your local nursery or the internet is a helpful resource for additional options.

Grasshoppers

When we first moved to Cheshire on the north end of Flagstaff in 1977, it was new tract housing in an open meadow. Grasshoppers were thick, a plague of Biblical proportions! I would go out in the morning to see hundreds of them on the walls of the house and on the wood fence. They were sunning themselves, getting energy to devour everything I had planted.

I have found little boys are the best defense against grasshoppers. All insects were protected on Cooper Drive. No killing spiders, they were carefully picked up with a Kleenex and taken outside. No using a magnifying glass to burn ants. No catching butterflies, leave the bees alone, lizards and snakes were strictly catch (play with for a short while) and release. But it was open season on grasshoppers and all options to kill them had my stamp of approval.

Grasshoppers taped to bicycle spokes made a nice clicking motorized sound. I looked out the window one day to see Shawn had impaled grasshoppers on the tips of the chain link fence providing a smörgåsbord for the birds! I myself had a gallon milk jug half filled with water and would pluck them off the walls and drop them in. When a sufficient number of grasshoppers had perished by drowning, I poured it out on the garden. I thought maybe they would get a disease, or at least be frightened and leave. Sometimes the kids used this method with soda pop cans. One day my daughter Lisa came home and saw a 7 UP can on the counter, "Great" she thought as she picked it up, "Someone left a half can of soda!" She took a gulp only to realize it was a "grasshopper smoothie".

My neighbor Kay recently reminisced about our grasshopper problem. "Remember when Shea and Robin built a fort out in the ditch?" I did remember the boys' fort. "They turned it into a 'Grasshopper

Museum' and they kept asking me to come see it. Finally, I went out there. It was disturbing." Kay recalled, "They had shelves in the fort and one shelf held grasshopper legs, another grasshopper wings, still another heads, all lined up neatly." She added, "Well, they all grew up, have responsible jobs and no one became a serial killer."

Even my brother-in-law Dennis, a big kid himself, experimented with microwaving grasshoppers. They explode in 15 seconds or less.

With further development and lots of shade trees, the grasshoppers have largely disappeared. All pests including grasshoppers will go for a sick or weakened plant. Keep your plants well-watered and cared for, keep down the weeds and provide a shady environment.

Slugs

If it's hot and dry you have grasshoppers, if it is cool and moist you have slugs. You can't win! Slugs were not a problem until the grasshoppers were gone. I have not had much luck with the beer method. I have "baited" them with lettuce leaves, the ones they had partially eaten. I set them out in the evening and wait a couple of hours. Then I go out with my flashlight and collect them, disposing of everything or just the slugs and re-bait with the leaves. They like to sleep under rocks, pots, or water containers. Locating their favorite sleeping places, you can collect them in the daytime.

Aphids

I hate aphids! A soap solution will work, spraying them with a strong spray on your hose works fairly well. I usually just squish them, sometimes with gloves and sometimes not. Although messy, there is satisfaction in this method. I told you I was cheap.

Ants

Generally, ants are not problematic. When they do become a problem, usually in a planter or in the compost, I shovel the ant hill or as much of it as I can get into a 5-gallon bucket of water and leave for about a week.

Mosquitoes

Mosquitoes won't bother your plants, but they will bother you and make garden chores miserable! For the last couple of years, we have had severe mosquito problems in Flagstaff. We have never had mosquito problems before! In the past they might be around for a little while in the evening, but these mosquitoes are all over town and are out from dawn till dark. After 100 bites, I put a "HELP" on Facebook to see if people had good ideas. Of course, the obvious is chemical insect repellent, but I don't want to use that in an organic garden. The best advice came from friends who live in Alaska and Canada. Basically, cover your skin! It kills me, but on "mosquito days" I wear long pants, two long sleeved shirts, hot pink, they don't like bright colors, a scarf, a hat and over the hat mosquito netting cover. I traded my nice mesh garden gloves for my Playtex dish-washing gloves. I'm hot and I can barely see but I'm not getting bit.

Gophers

Customers would come to my farmstand lamenting their plight with gophers. I tried to be sympathetic but I had never laid eyes on one. Occasionally, when I was particularly obnoxious, I would say, "I have prayed against them." Jesus thought I was getting smug, needed a new life lesson, and should have more empathy with my customers. So He sent me, and most of Flagstaff, with a gopher plague. They seemed to come out of nowhere, dropped from heaven overnight. I was horrified at the destruction they were causing. Peas disappeared. Beans could be seen wiggling in broad daylight and then they were gone! Mounds appeared in the middle of my asparagus beds and I knew they were eating the roots.

I went to my neighbor, Tom, who is a research biologist. I knew he had experience and would know what to do. "Tom, I have gophers everywhere. What can I do?" Tom, knowing what an animal lover I am, chose his words carefully, "Well, there is really only one way to deal with them: a "Maccabee" trap- but it kills them, and it is rather gruesome." Tom braced himself for what he was sure would be a protest to PLEASE find another way. I shocked him when I replied, "Good. I want to see their lifeless, dead bodies." Tom burst out laughing and then with a big grin, said, "That's not very 'Christian.'" "No," I said. "And it's not very 'Julie' either, but I want them GONE!"

Tom set up the trap for me while I took my three grandsons, six-year-old twins and a four-year-old, who were staying with me to the Aqua-plex. They wanted to "close it down" so it was after dark when we got home. "Let's go check the trap!" I said. Sure enough, we had one! Two of the boys were squealing with delight and the third was crying because he didn't get to see it pulled out. We were making so much noise the neighbors came out to see what was going on.

There were gophers in the backyard of the rental house next door. I could see the mounds through the chain link fence. I couldn't set traps in their yard, but they did have a cat. Snow, as his name implies, is a large, extremely friendly cat and like most cats, he spent most of the day sleeping. His favorite spot was the middle of the road where he would sprawl out absorbing the heat from the black asphalt. I would look out the window to see two cars going in opposite directions stopped in the street. I knew exactly what was going on! I would go out to retrieve him so traffic could resume. One day, I sat down, put him in my lap, pet him and talked to him, "Snow, you have got to get with it buddy and start catching gophers. I bet they are tasty! Snow, you're a cat, you are supposed to catch things- but not birds, just gophers." I proceeded to pray for him, "Jesus, please turn this cat into a gopher hunter, I need all the help I can get!" By the end of the summer, Tom had caught five, and Snow had caught six! Of course, Snow proudly deposited the mostly eaten gophers on his owner's back step.

As effective as the Maccabee trap is for catching gophers, it requires more strength than I have to set it or release it. As helpful as Tom was, he has better things to do than set gopher traps, like teach classes at the University and do research. He suggested I use poison. "Oh no, I am too afraid I will kill something else, like a hawk, or an owl, or a fox or a dog." Tom assured me that poison directed at gophers and put into their tunnel would only kill them. "The gopher ingests the poison in the tunnel, it is fast acting and it will die in there. Nothing is desperate enough to dig up a dead gopher." With that encouragement, I went to my local Ace Hardware/Home-Co store and talked to the very helpful garden guy, whose name was also Tom. He really had a GREAT suggestion. The "yard butler", about $30 is easy to use and very effective. It looks much like a pogo stick. Gopher poison is sold with it and comes in a pellet form. You find the tunnel by poking around near the mounds of dirt. Once the pointed stick plunges through, you know you have it. By releasing a lever, you distribute the poison into the tunnel. Tom suggested once the poison is distributed, putting a rock over the hole so the gopher does not see daylight. It is important to stay on this as gophers multiply very quickly and they can and will destroy a yard and garden! Gophers move around a lot in the fall so that is when you are likely to see fresh mounds. They also use existing tunnels from deceased gophers. Yuck!

Squirrels

I have a friend who has made a career out of live-trapping animals. I attended a workshop on pests and the wildlife biologist did not recommend it. He said it makes us feel better to live trap but in the end it could be less humane. An animal dropped off in the woods is not welcomed by the animals already living there. They may not be able to find food or water and could starve, or be a meal. It also doesn't always work. A man in Camp Verde was live trapping squirrels. The squirrel(s) began to look familiar and he suspected he might be catching the same one over and over. He had a can of hot pink spray paint, so he painted the tail and took the squirrel three miles down the road. Two weeks later, a squirrel with a pink tail appeared in his yard!

Rabbits and Chipmunks

Last week, I saw a rabbit hopping in the yard across the street. I moaned. The paragraph in this edition is blissfully short, and I sincerely hope I don't have a rabbit story for the next edition. Plant flowers and vegetables in raised beds, pots, or animal troughs, which are my favorite. Put chicken wire at the bottom of beds and around young trees.

Skunks

Occasionally they get into the compost or take a bite out of your squash. They are watching the same strawberry you are watching, and I guarantee they will get it hours or minutes before you planned to pick it. I leave them alone.

Deer

It is best to have a 6-foot-high chain link fence around your garden and plant things in your perennial bed they don't like, such as daffodils and irises. Deer come through the neighborhood ditch fairly often. They will eat my chard if desperate. They won't eat my squash, asparagus, rhubarb or green beans. They ate all the lettuce of one neighbor and all the corn of another.

Elk

Don't plant a garden.

Beneficials

Let's end on a positive note! There are beneficial things living in your garden that can be fully appreciated.

Bees

I have thousands of native bees and have never been stung in my own yard. They know me! I can even pet them, although they don't like it. Having a constant and continual supply of flowers from early spring to late fall guarantees lots of happy bees!

Lady Bugs

Some years they are in abundance and some years they aren't. I like to purchase the containers of them at the nursery just because they are so fun to watch. They are good to buy when the aphid population is out of control.

Moths

Moths are night pollinators and very beneficial. They are also beautiful and fun to watch.

Bats

Another night pollinator, and they eat a ton of insects! Read up on bats and you will be surprised at what great little creatures they are. Scary movies have done them a real injustice.

Garter Snakes

Garter snakes eat slugs and other insects and are your garden's friend. They are harmless. Babies are born live in mid-summer and are adorable!

If you are lucky enough to have toads, frogs, mosquito hawks or spiders in your yard, they are all working hard to rid your yard of the damaging insects.

CHAPTER 10: TOOLS OF THE TRADE

Since gardening is such a popular hobby, you can be sure there are those vigorously trying to sell you products and services, most of which you don't need. I have purchased very few tools through retail outlets. Electrical or motorized tools tend to scare me. I enjoy doing everything by hand. For some of you, the FUN is in garden gadgets; automatic sprinkler or drip systems, rototillers, chipper shredders, riding mowers, cold frames, greenhouses and hoop houses- to name a few. If this is you, go for it!

Here is a list of simple tools for the garden:

Essential Tools

- Shovel- I prefer the short-handled one, because I am short easier for me to handle.
- Garden fork- heavy duty with thick tines. A garden fork is a smaller version of a pitchfork.
- Leaf Rake- thin, flexible, aluminum tines.
- Yard Rake-heavy-duty steel tines.
- Trowel or hand-shovel- you can't have too many of these. I buy every one I see at garage sales, as I like to have several around the yard. I am always misplacing them.
- Dandelion Digger
- Hand clipper- good quality! I have purchased all my good clippers, paying at least $30/pair. This is one item not to go cheap on; the same goes for flower shears or clippers.
- Large Clipper-for small limbs and shrubs.
- Wheelbarrow- a size you can easily manage. I like the smaller plastic ones as I can barely move the big steel ones even when they are empty.
- Five Gallon Buckets
- Compost Bin(s)- these are usually converted garbage cans with an 80-gallon capacity. I have used plastic garbage cans with the bottom cut out as well.
- Gloves- I am obsessive about protecting my hands. Dirt under the fingernails is not fun. Working in the yard, my hands are cut, cracked and bleeding in no-time. So, I take a little extra

care to protect my hands.

- Try A&D ointment, olive oil or cocoa butter
- Use cotton gloves
- When using latex, vinyl, or rubber gloves (for washing dishes), I double-layer, pulling the cotton ones out to let them dry as my hands get sweaty. For safety, don't use heavier work gloves when you will be in dirt or water, pulling weeds or trimming.

Other Items

- Child paint brushes or Q-Tips- for pollinating
- Coffee filters- to line pots
- Clothes pins- all sorts of uses
- Laundry baskets- to cover tender plants during frost. I have found that these are the best protection for young squash plants (T&E). They nest easily and can be brought out only when you need them. For severe cold, cover the basket with a sheet.
- Teaspoon or baby spoon- to use for seedling transplant
- Bucket of mid-sized rocks- these are handy to hold down plastic or support a plant
- Saucers
- Stakes- bamboo, wood, or metal stakes of all sizes

Watering

- 2-3 Watering cans- think recycling! Plastic gallon milk jugs with the top sliced off are good for dipping water out of large containers such as collection bins below gutters. I usually have at least 10-20 of these around the yard.
- Plastic garbage cans or bins for water collection or storage- I have one under every downspout, and several in the yard and ditch for easy watering.

Seeds

I buy all of my seeds from mail order catalogs* where I find a great variety. After ordering early, the seeds arrive in January, allowing me to start my garden while the snow still covers the ground and temperatures drop below freezing.

Catalogs offer larger quantities of seeds. A small packet of beans in a retail outlet will run between $1.30-$4. Mail order catalogs may sell a half-pound of seeds for $6-$7. This bag of beans will last through several growing seasons. Seeds generally don't go "bad", although the retail stores would like you to think so. Each year stored, seed germination percentage may drop, requiring the gardener to plant a few extras. I once found a whole bag of seed packets in the trash that were fifteen years old. I had no idea where they had been kept or how they had been stored. Eighteen squash seeds germinated in one of the packets. The flowers and other vegetables all had great germination rates as well!

Some gardeners arrange to share an order with another gardener or trade seeds. One person may buy beans while the other will buy peas. When first trying a new vegetable or flower, it is often best to start with a small packet to ensure that you like growing it and that the plant does well. Some items don't warrant a large packet of seed.

Books

I have been very pleased with anything by Eliot Coleman. I have worn thin his book, "The New Organic Gardener". Barbara Damrosch's book, "The Garden Primer", is a complete guide on almost everything you would need to know about gardening and the resource book I go to first with any question.

CHAPTER 11: EVERYTHING I NEED FOR THE GARDEN, I FOUND IN THE TRASH

You can spend a fortune at the local nursery or home improvement store when paying full price for everything from plants to soil and pots. I prefer the TREASURE HUNT, known as bulky trash day. This is the designated day that neighborhoods set out their "too big for the can" items on the curb for the Sanitation department to pick up. At first, I limited myself to bags of leaves, always going at night. Then, I moved to early morning, disguising myself with a hat and long coat. Now, I mark the day on the calendar, inspecting the offerings in broad daylight. I freely talk about my treasures with anyone who will listen-just short of bragging about my discoveries!

So for the record, last year I found:

- 2 birdbaths
- 2 compost bins
- 1 wrought iron spiral plant holder
- 1 trellis
- 3 hoses in perfect condition
- Numerous large, black plastic pots
- Terracotta pots
- Potting soil in pots
- Bag of unopened potting soil
- Hanging baskets
- Live petunias
- A wheelbarrow
- Air-mattress (to cover compost)
- Seeds
- Several plant stands
- Tomato cages

This is not to mention what I found for myself and for my grand-children:

- 3 bikes, a dresser, a doll house, a slide, clothes, dolls and toys, a record player for my niece and a bread machine for my son. Both had requested these items the week before!

I go to the older, middle-income, established neighborhoods for the best "bulky trash" results. The more expensive the house, the less likely the chance of finding anything good. I concentrate on my own neighborhood, but if I am in another area of town, I don't hesitate to scrounge. Legally, once an item is set on the curb, it is open season, fair game! The other advantage to the great treasure hunt is in keeping recyclable items out of the landfill. I often pick up things with the intention of depositing them in my recycle bin.

Garage Sales

Here is another great place to pick up garden items, especially garden tools. I buy every trowel I see, usually for as little as 25 cents. I need a lot of them, mostly because I misplace them. I like to have them in a number of places in the yard- trowels are the tool I use most.

At moving sales, inquire about pots, Miracle-Gro fertilizer or other items you are interested in. I find that in asking for the 6-pack or quart-sized pots, people say, "Oh, I have a whole box of those. I didn't think anyone would want them." The same is often true with Miracle-Gro or other garden products as I hear, "I do have that. I forgot about those bottles." Many people will give these products away or at a low price. Craigslist, and other similar neighborhood sites and apps are great resources for finding used items useful in the garden.

Ask Around

Finally, let people know what items you hope to find. After the Christmas holiday, I'll advertise: Unwanted plants wanted, dead or alive, no questions asked!" I get lots of stuff. Poinsettias are especially good as they come in a nice pot with good potting soil, foil and a bow.

Some plants can be revived, while others are gone for good! If I'm concerned with a dead or dying plant about spores in the soil or an insect infestation, I'll leave the pot outside to freeze for a number of nights. This usually guarantees that any pathogens are dead. Since I use this soil to start geraniums, this has never been a problem. We sell the plants at the church garage sale or our annual craft sale with proceeds going to world-wide missions.

Roxi and the Bulky Trash

Monday, August 25, 2010, 5:30 a.m.

I was up and out the door to see what wonderful treasures God had provided for me this month on Bulky Trash day. Bulky Trash is once a month where residents in Flagstaff can set larger items out for pick-up which are too "bulky" to fit into the regular trash can.

I put Roxi, my son Shawn's four-year-old rescue dog in the car, threw the keys onto the driver's seat and ran back into the house to get my coffee cup. I came back out and the door was locked. Roxi had locked herself in the car! Panic set in. I'm not sure if the panic was over time lost in the bulky trash treasure hunt, or the fear of Roxi eventually suffocating, or both! I had a spare key, I wondered where it was. I hadn't' seen it in five years.

I opened Shawn's bedroom door, "Shawn, get up! Roxi locked herself in the car!"

"MOM! What time is it?! Call a locksmith."

"Shawn, I don't want to call a locksmith. If I have to pay $25 to unlock the car door, it completely defeats the purpose of looking for free stuff in the trash!" Eventually, I decided I had no other option, so okay, I will call my friend, Vic, from Flag Lock and Key. I called Vic's cellphone and was treated to a rap song on his answering machine, "I changed the lock on my front door, you can't come here anymore, and you can't come into my house and you can't lay down on my couch!"

"Hey, Vic. This is Julie McDonald, I'm so sorry it's so early. It's an emergency, my dog locked herself in the car, call me."

I went back inside to tell Shawn, "Vic didn't answer, maybe he is on vacation, should I call the police?" I know they will come for a kid, would they come for a dog?

"Mom, don't call the police, they will just tell you to call a locksmith." "I did call a locksmith!" "Call another one! If you get me a wire hanger, I might be able to open the door."

I wondered why my 19-year-old son knew how to open a door with a wire hanger, but I told myself I would think about that later. Thousands of wire hangers had circulated through the house over the last 30 years. Could I find one? NO.

I waited a few more minutes to see if Vic called me back. Maybe, if I can get Roxi excited, she will step on the key and unlock the door! I ran inside and got her leash, dangled it over the window on the passenger's side. Roxi sat up and wagged her tail. Oh! A car ride AND a walk! I ran back in and got her treat box and dangled it over the window. Roxi stopped wagging her tail, tilted her head and looked at me as if to say, "You are acting strange. Am I safe riding with you?"

Excited wasn't working. Roxi needs to be agitated so she would jump around and then maybe accidentally step on the key. I had an idea- a cat! Cats get Roxi agitated! Bad idea, cats are hard to catch, and they were all still sleeping.

Willow, the neighbor's dog will get Roxi worked up. I ran across the street and looked in the Peterson's entrance way. All the lights were off in the kitchen. I couldn't wake people up to borrow their dog!

The sun was fairly high now, and it was starting to get warm. I looked in the car and Roxi was curled up in the passenger's seat, eyes half closed, bored to death with my antics.

Just then, my neighbor from down the street, Diana, came peddling by. She was out for an early morning bike ride with her dog, Panda. PERFECT! I called out, "Diana, stop! I need to borrow your dog!" She slammed on her brakes, jumped off of her bike and said, "Okay, what do you want my dog for?" I said, "Roxi locked herself in the car, I need you to run around the car in circles with Panda to get Roxi worked up, and maybe she will step on the key and unlock the door." Diana graciously embraced this idea with gusto and before long, Panda was indeed running around in circles, and Roxi was up from her nap, barking furiously! This went on for a good five minutes. I stood by the car door and prayed, "Jesus, please help me! Let the dog's foot hit the keys just right."

CLICK.

The door unlocked, I opened it, and Roxi jumped out, and attacked Panda! Diana and I threw our arms around each other, celebrating success! Shawn came out and said, "Mom, you are going to wake up the whole neighborhood!"

I ran back into the house and called Vic to tell him the dog had unlocked the door. Vic was just starting his van, on his way to my rescue.

6:15 a.m., a late start for bulky trash. While I was driving, I reflected back on the time Mike had locked himself in the car. I had walked Lisa into her gymnastics class, and when I walked out, I found Mike, two-years-old, had gotten out of his car seat, gone to all the doors and locked them and was jumping and hopping from seat to seat, pointing and laughing just like a monkey. All I could do was stand there and laugh! I knew the police would come if I had to call them, and it was winter, so I had time. He eventually unlocked the doors.

God did bless me again with a great bulky trash, too! I got a fire pit which I sold twice, a bike that I sold at a wedding, a table for the conversation corner, and a carload of pots, planters, potting soil, and yard tools. The only problem with that great find was that I got there at the same time as the bulky trash pick-up men. That is what happens when you're late! I begged, "Wait guys, I want some of that." They helped me load it and one of them said he "knew" me. He said, "Yeah, people throw out such good stuff. If we could pull a trailer, we could have a yard sale every week with the stuff we find." Of course they can't, but maybe…

CHAPTER 12: GARDENING WITH CHILDREN

Expose your children to gardening! Sometimes this works, developing a life-long passion for gardening. Sometimes it doesn't. At age thirty-two, the only garden flower my daughter, Lisa, can name correctly, is the tulip. My son, Mike, loved gardening from the start and won numerous awards at the county fair. He can still name almost every plant in any garden. Joey had zero interest. I happened to walk outside in the front yard just in time to hear a frustrated eleven-year-old Mike trying to educate his reluctant six-year-old brother. "Joey, what is that flower?"

Mike pointed to a Veronica. Joey looked blank. He obviously didn't know the answer. Mike offered a hint, "It starts with a 'v.'" "Virgin?" asked Joey.

With that, Mike got on his bike and rode off. To my knowledge, that was the end of Joey's floricultural education. Shawn, my youngest son, loved being IN the garden! His interest was bugs, snakes, and his "pet" spiders or whatever creature he might find under the rocks.

Encourage children by giving their own small area where they can plant a few of the hardiest plants. I suggest that if they want to try the harder varieties, tell them, "If what you grow this year does well, and you take care of it, then you can try that next year."

Davis, 5, *helping harvest basil.*

I recommend day lilies for future flower lovers. They are indestructible, easy and enjoyable for children to grow. I have one large clump of lilies that never bloomed for ten years. They WOULD have bloomed but they were laid on or used for games of hide and seek. Bikes were thrown on top of them, the dogs roamed through them. They survived all of the abuse!

Children enjoy planting bulbs. Bulbs are useful to teach delayed gratification! Crocus, grape hyacinths, tulips, 'Glory of the Snow', and daffodils are all good. I would especially recommend the crocus as they are up so early and the daffodil because they are practically guaranteed to bloom each year. Planting the bulbs in an area on the south side, near the house, is good as the children are able to enjoy watching them emerge as early as January.

Julia helping Mimi plant seeds and bulbs.

With annual flowers, children enjoy cosmos, nasturtiums, and sunflowers. Both the nasturtiums and sunflowers begin with fairly large seeds, easier for small fingers to handle. Children enjoy the heady results of a large sunflower at eye level as they bloom.

As for vegetables, every child should grow pumpkins at least once. What a great variety they have to choose from in considering that will be the biggest or the best! Girls might like the miniature pumpkins and boys might like the giant pumpkin varieties. I really like the old heirloom, New England pie pumpkin, as its name implies this nice size variety is great for pies. Children with active imaginations will also enjoy the gourds. Remember to soak the seeds on both the pumpkins and gourds for better germination.

Kara's bouquet from Mimi's garden.

Beans are another good "kid" vegetable. My twin grandsons, at age two, were able to plant several pots by themselves. The seeds are easy for them to handle. The plants grow fast to satisfy their shorter attention spans. They find it fun to grow green, purple, and yellow varieties together. Pole beans are fun, when grown over a "tee-pee" frame of twine, creating a little "fort" for the kids to play in as the vines creep up the poles.

I've often wondered why so

many adults want children to grow radishes. Why? The reward for all their time, watering and watching, is something that I consider to taste terrible!

As the plants begin to mature, allowing the children to help water other areas of the garden is always fun. Let them cut some flowers for bouquets. I have been careful to leave the garden chore of weeding until they are older and able to distinguish between the weeds and

The twins, Jason and Trenton, watering a geranium.

seedlings (T&E). Fortunately, I enjoy weeding even if many people do not.

Harvesting is the reward for all of us, so be sure to include your kids in this activity. The time spent, investing in a child, pays off in great rewards. Gardening builds relationships and character. My son, Mike, built all of the beds behind my house. Of course, it wasn't totally due to his love of gardening. He was usually working off being grounded. We still have a great relationship, in and out of the garden.

CHAPTER 13: WHAT TO DO WITH ALL OF THE PRODUCE?

So, you've invested the time into your garden. Plants are growing leaps and bounds; produce is hanging from the plants. You're successful! Now what?

Worrying about what you are going to do with excess produce is like wondering what you would do if you had a million dollars! Wait until it happens, then worry about it! There are so many options, believe me, this won't be a problem.

- You can freeze it. Here is a great tip I got from an eighty-year-old farmer for freezing squash and many other vegetables. Slice or cube it, then spread it onto a cookie sheet with the pieces not touching. Place the pans in the freezer. When they are frozen, remove with a spatula and put in freezer bags for storage.

- Dehydrate or dry them.

- Take vegetables to church. I have sold vegetables at church for years for various mission projects. It is a great treat for all of the people that don't have gardens. Set out a small container for the money you will collect from purchases, checking it after the event.

- Take it to work. Maybe there is an employee who has a need. People can donate toward helping with that need and get some fresh veggies.

I put a reasonable price on the vegetables and flowers for sale. If you put "donation" only, people are very reluctant to pick things up. They are not sure what "donation" is acceptable, and they hesitate. Setting a price is helpful to them. More often than not, they put more than the given price.

Don't want to bother with money? You can give it away. Set it out on a table with a "free" sign. I prefer this to giving people a bag of veggies. People never refuse a bag, but they may not like what you are giving them. When it's set out, they can take what they want and the amount they'll use.

Trade veggies! I trade veggies for the delicious baked goods from my neighbor, Kay. We're both happy! Another lady happily trades organic eggs for my produce.

Donate it to a soup kitchen or a local shelter.

The Neighborhood Farmstand: for Entertainment ONLY!

My goal was always to have excess vegetables so I could sell them. First, I set them on a counter at church with a small collection tin, donating the proceeds to mission projects. When I turned 50, I asked myself, "What do I want to do to celebrate my 50th year? What have I never done?

I wanted to have a Farmstand! So, that summer, I began preparations for my first Farmstand. My kids laughed at me throughout the summer. And, as my daughter told me a few years later, "Mom, we're still laughing."

The first year, in August, as the garden began to produce, I set out a white board and computer desk (of course I found it in the bulky trash). I only had some beans and squash along with the payment can. The first day, I made $2. I was so I excited, I hung the money on the refrigerator where it remained for the rest of the year!

Every year, the stand got bigger. My husband made a beautiful garden cart with a roof out of a discarded bicycle baby carrier. I started selling lettuce with edible flowers; I offered chard, kale, and cherry tomatoes. People came in droves! One year, someone asked me what I had the most of, and I truthfully answered, "Customers!"

Surprisingly, the favorite item is squash. Everyone wants squash. Many say it is the most beautiful squash they have ever seen.

I love running the Farmstand, as I have so much fun with it. I have met so many great people and made many new friends. One day, three women were chatting away at the Farmstand, when a couple came by. After listening for a few minutes, the husband observed, "You all must be good friends."

They looked at each other, started laughing, and said, "Well, we know each other from the Farmstand!"

As the fall season arrives and the garden draws to a close, I usually break down and cry as I begin to put everything away. I've had so much fun and now it's over for the year. But along with all of those sports fans, I say, "Wait until next year, bigger and better!"

*Seed Catalogs

There is an abundance of wonderful catalogs out there! I find it best to select a few that are good for your own purpose and buy from them. Shipping
and handling costs will become unreasonable if you order from too many
companies. You may miss out on bulk discounts or special offers if your order is small. I often stagger orders, ordering a lot from a particular catalog
one year, then a lot from a different catalog the next year.

Harris Seeds
Box 24966
Rochester, NY 14624
www.harrisseds.com

Most of my seeds come from this fine catalog. They are based in New York
State and sell to both professional growers and home gardeners. They have
customer service, and as I mentioned in the sunflower section, their resident
farm, Jeff Werner, is an exceptional resource.

Pinetree Garden Seeds
Box 300
New Glouster, ME 04260
207-926-3400

Based in Maine, with growing conditions similar to Flagstaff, I order frequently from this catalog. They have a great lettuce mix. They also offer a
great variety of smaller packages of seeds at a very reasonable price. This
catalog is great to try new varieties to see how they do in your garden.

Henry Fields
Box 397
Aurora, IN 47001
513-354-1494

This nursery has a great variety of vegetables and flower seeds offered at
good prices. I can buy seeds like beans and squash in bulk and get a very reasonable price. I have been pleased with the perennials I have ordered from
them. Henry Fields and Gurneys have very similar catalogs, and I believe are
both under the same parent company.

Totally Tomatoes

I have not personally ordered from this company, but most of my gardening friends do. They are very pleased with the seeds they have received. They
seem to be the most complete source for tomatoes and peppers.

Netherlands Bulb Company
13 McFadden Road
Easton, PA 18045
www.netherlandbulb.com

For spring flowering bulbs, including tulips, daffodils and crocus, I have
been very happy with Netherland Bulb. If you can hold off until later in the
year, or after January 1, you can pick up some great sales from them. They
also sell in bulk quantities for additional savings.

Acknowledgments

To my grandmother, Mathilda Benson, 1870-1963, whose life has always inspired me.

My dad, Verner Gustav (Spud) Benson, 1914-1981, humorous writer and cartoonist. A great dad, who encouraged me in every endeavor and taught me to garden.

To my brother-in-law, Dennis McDonald, better than a real brother, entertaining, helpful in lots of ways and making me laugh for over 40 years. He WILL be in my next book!

My friend, David Menne, from whom I have gleaned numerous valuable gardening tips for over 30 years.

My wonderful neighbors for over 40 years, Tom and Kay Whitham. They are the BEST neighbors in the whole world! Tom, who was raised on a tree farm in Iowa, is a research biologist and a veritable fountain of garden information. Kay can do wonders with my veggies in the kitchen. I grow, she cooks- we are both happy!

My four, great kids, Lisa, Mike, Joey, and Shawn, who all helped dragging, carrying, moving, lifting, loading, and planting. Making lots of fun of mom, but also very encouraging.

John Winnicki for more truckloads of manure than I can count.

Jim Mast for his helpful seminars, who is very approachable and willing to share his garden expertise. I first met Jim at the Coconino County Fair, a great place to learn about flowers and vegetables.

Thanks to my wonderful editor, Randi Diskin, for doing all of the typing of the book, taking photos, editing and putting it all together. If I live to be 100, I will never be able to thank you enough for all you have done for me!

Photos:

Collecting photos was a team effort between my iPhone, my friends, Julianne Ksiazek and Randi Diskin.

BOOKS BY JULIE McDONALD

*All books are available as eBooks for. 99 cents on Amazon. Read fr free with KindleUnlimited. *Print books are available at various Arizc retailers or through Amazon for $10.00*
Many also available in audiobook format at major retailers!

ARIZONA AND PIONEER HISTORY

- Unbreakable Dolls*
- Unbreakable Dolls, Too*
- Three Cheers for Unbreakab le Dolls*
- Saints & Scoundrels: Colorful Characters of Arizona*
- Saints & Scoundrels: Colorful Characters of the Grand Canyon*
- Saints & Scoundrels: Colorful Characters of the American West
- Tails from the Grand Canyon

SINGLE STORY EBOOKS

Concise, 10-40 pages, with great historic and contemporary color photos

- The 1931 Trunk Murders: The Story of Winnie Ruth Judd
- Elizabeth Heiser: Cattle Rancher & Cougar
- Last Drink: The Almost Unbelievable Story of John Shaw
- The Murderous Madam
- Honeymoon Disappearance: Glen & Bessie Hyde's 1928 River Raft Trip Through Grand Canyon
- Philip Johnston and the Navajo Code Talkers
- Climax Jim: Arizona's Lovable Outlaw
- Marguerite Brunswig Staude: Building the Chapel of the Holy Cross, Sedona, Arizona
- Mary Bickerdyke: Civil War Heroine
- Donaldina Cameron: Rescuing Chinese Girls from the Sex-Slave Trade in 1900's San Francisco
- Evalyn Walsh McLean and the Curse of the Hope Diamond
- Emily Griffith and the Opportun ity School in Denver, Colorado
- Irene Aloha Wright: Traveler, Researcher and International Writer
- Sedona: Beautiful Woman, Beautiful Town

And many more!

www.funhistorystories.com

Heroes in Black History

- Clara Brown: The Rags to Riches Story of a Freed Slave
- Negro Bill of Moab, Utah
- "Stagecoach" Mary Fields
- The Genius of Barney Ford: Escaped Slave, Entrepreneur, Activist of Breckenridge, Colorado
- The True Story of Bass Reeves, U.S. Deputy Marshall
- Harriet Beecher Stowe: The Little Lady Who Started the Civil War
- Susan Angeline Collins
- George Washington Carver: Man of God, Man of Purpose
- Black Professionals of the Old American West
- The True Story of Freed Slave Jim Beckwourth: Mountain Man, Trapper, Explorer, Chief of the Mountain Crow

Underground Railroad

- Tales From the Underground Railroad
- Tales From the Underground Railroad, Too
- Slave Girls on the Run
- A Slave's Courtroom Drama: The Remarkable Story of Louis
- Levi Coffin: President and Conductor on the Underground Railroad
- Actors on Board: A Slave's Performance of a Lifetime
- Aunt Rachel's Miraculous Escape

And many more! www.funhistorystories.com

Books by Julie McDonald Continued

Truth Behind Tradition eBooks

- The True Story of Saint Patrick of Ireland
- The True Story of Saint Valentine of Terni, Italy
- The True Story of John Chapman "Johnny Appleseed" an American Folk Hero
- The True Story of Squanto and the First Thanksgiving
- The True Story of Saint Nicholas of Myra, Turkey of the Mediterranean Sea
- The True Story of Saint Francis of Assisi, Italy

Christian eBooks

- Adventures in Freedom: 10 Steps to Forgiveness
- Adventures in Giving
- Adventures in Prayer
- The Prison Song: The Story of Art Carrera

Gardening

- Farm Your Front Yard*
- Growing and Selling Daffodils
- Growing and Selling Rhubarb

Book Combos $1.99 on Amazon

Unbreakable Dolls Trilogy

Unbreakable Dolls of the Midwest

Arizona Outlaws

And many more!

www.funhistorystories.com